BHARAT

Leading Yesterday - Leading Tomorrow

DR LAL TANWANI

INDIA • SINGAPORE • MALAYSIA

ISBN 979-8-89475-615-8

Table of Contents

Introduction

Dr. Lal N. Tanwani: A Life Dedicated to Learning and Teaching

My name is Dr. Lal N. Tanwani, but many know me as Lal Sir. I have dedicated my life to the pursuit of knowledge and academic excellence. Over the years, I have earned recognition for holding the most educational degrees by an individual, as recorded by the World Book of Records London, Asia Book of Records, International Book of World Records Bravo, and India Book of Records.

My academic journey began in 1991, and it has been a diverse and enriching experience. My qualifications include:

- B.Com.
- M.Com. (Finance)
- B.Ed.
- M.Com. (Cost Accounts)
- M.A. (Economics)
- M.Phil. (Commerce)
- Ph.D. (Commerce)
- MBA (Finance)
- Advanced Diploma in Value Education
- D.Litt
- Ph.D. (Management)

These degrees reflect my commitment to continuous learning and my desire to gain a comprehensive understanding across various disciplines.

In addition to my personal academic achievements, I am deeply involved in education and entrepreneurship. As the CEO of Padma Coaching Classes and the Director of Programs at the Padma Institute of Knowledge & Research, I strive to empower students in their academic pursuits. I am also the Founder Trustee of NCT Convent School and BBRT International School, as well as the Director of Nav Jeevan Co-Op Bank Ltd. My institutions focus on nurturing talent in commerce, banking, finance, and management.

In 2024, I established Padma International Preschool, where we blend the British curriculum with Indian values and heritage. Here, we train students with essential skills from the age of three.

My passion for education extends beyond the classroom. I have actively participated in numerous conferences and workshops, both nationally and internationally, advocating for continuous learning. With over 30 years of teaching experience, I have honed my skills to meet the needs of students in fast-paced environments, always maintaining the highest degree of integrity and confidentiality.

My story is one of dedication, perseverance, and an unrelenting pursuit of knowledge. I hope to inspire students and educators alike, demonstrating that learning is a lifelong journey that knows no boundaries.

Awards and Achievements

Throughout my career, I have been honored with numerous awards, both in India and internationally. Some of my notable accolades include:

- International Book of World Records Bravo 2023
- "Maximum Educational Degrees Achieved by An Individual" by India Book of Records 2021
- "Grandmaster Certification" by Asia Book of Records 2021
- "Maximum Educational Degrees Held by an Individual" by World Book of Records, London 2021
- "Nelson Mandela Nobel Peace Award 2020" for Education & Social Activist
- "Certificate of Excellence 2020" for "Global Peace For Making India Sustainable Developed & Strong" by The American University
- 2019 Indo Asia Award for Excellence in Education, Dubai (U.A.E.)
- "International Achievers Award 2018 for Education Excellence", Thailand
- "Award for Outstanding Research Paper" by University of Mumbai 2018
- Dr. A. P. J. Abdul Kalam Lifetime Achievement Award 2018 from International Institute for Social & Economic Reforms, Bengaluru
- ET Business Icons by Neil Nitin Mukesh in 2020
- Citation Award 2018 for Best Teacher from University of Mumbai
- Bharat Ratna Dr. Radhakrishan Gold Medal Award 2018, Chennai
- Shiksha Bharati Award 2017, New Delhi
- "Best Teaching Award 2017" by Indian Education Awards, Delhi

Positions Held

Over the years, I have held several significant positions:

- Founder Trustee of BBRT International School
- Founder Trustee of N.C.T. Convent School, Ulhasnagar
- Founder of Jaywanti Notandas Tanwani Charitable Trust
- CEO of Padma Coaching Classes
- Director of Programs at the Padma Institute of Knowledge & Research
- Director in The Nav – Jeevan Co-op Bank Ltd.
- Past Educational Director of Jhulelal Trust School, Ulhasnagar
- Past President of Rotary Club of Ulhasnagar Midtown
- Past President of Lion's Club, Ulhasnagar

- Lecturer at Oriental Institute of Management, Vashi
- Lecturer at Birla College, Kalyan

My journey is a testament to the transformative power of education. I hope to inspire others to pursue knowledge and personal growth with the same passion and dedication.

8 ◆ Introduction

- Lecturer at Oriental Institute of Management, Vashi
- Lecturer at Birla College, Kalyan

My journey is a testament to the transformative power of education. I hope to inspire others to pursue knowledge and personal growth with the same passion and dedication.

Introduction to Vedic Culture

An unknown fact about India is that the contribution of its early civilization has rarely been part of academic education. Let's understand the outstanding Vedic culture of India and its supreme contribution to the entire world, which still exists in its own way. Hindu culture is renowned for its spirituality. However, science, technology, and industry are also deeply connected with this culture.

The reason people are unaware of other facts about Hindu culture is that, according to recent research by Shri Dharampal and other renowned authors, colonial rulers wanted to destroy all positive aspects of Hindu culture. By the end of the 18th century, India was the world's industrial workshop. Hindus began with the basic principles of astronomy, fundamental particles, the origin of the universe, practical psychotherapy, etc., which are not well-documented and popularly known.

Ancient Hindus had highly developed technologies in textile engineering, ceramics, printing, weaponry, climatology and meteorology, architecture, medicine and surgery, metallurgy, agriculture and agricultural engineering, civil engineering, urban planning, and other fields, which are hardly known now. Another fact is that Hindus had extensive knowledge about the sun being the center of the solar system, the geography of the Earth, how plants produce food, how blood circulates in the body, principles of science, mathematics and numbers, health, medicine, and surgery, etc.

This valuable culture and great Indian civilization have been recognized by great foreign authors and literati. Arab scholar Sa'id ibn Ahmad al-Andalusi (1029-1070) wrote in his history of science, called Tabaqat-al-Umam:

"India was the first nation to launch science... India is known for the intelligence of its people. Over many centuries, all kings of the past recognized the capacity of Indians in all branches of knowledge."

American professor Jabez T. Sunderland (1842-1936), chairman of the India Information Bureau of America, spent many years in India. He was the author of "India in Bondage," in which he wrote,

"India began all sciences and brought some of them to a remarkable degree of development, leading the world. India has produced great literature, great arts, great philosophical systems, great religions, and great individuals in every department of life - rulers, statesmen, financiers, scholars, poets, colonizers, skilled artisans and craftsmen of all kinds, agriculturists, industrial organizers, and pioneers in far-reaching trade and commerce."

Its textile goods - fine products of its loom in cotton, wool, linen, and silk - were famous in the civilized world; so were its beautiful jewelry and precious stones, cut in every lovely form; pottery, porcelain of every kind, quality, color, and beautiful shape; fine work in iron, steel, silver, and gold. Its architecture was excellent.

Popular American author Mark Twain also had a high opinion of India and wrote,

"It had the first accumulation of material wealth; it was full of deep thinkers and intellectuals; it had mines, forests, and fertile soil."

Dick Teresi also acknowledges that the knowledge we understand today did not necessarily come from Greek civilization but was indeed present in India's Vedic traditions long before.

"Bishop Heber said: 'Of all the people I have met, Hindus are the bravest, wisest, most patient, and most eager for knowledge and improvement.'"

Contributions to Mathematics

Many people do not realize that ancient India is the cradle of great mathematical development. The early achievements from Vedic civilization have given us the pleasures we enjoy today. Chinese scholar and author Lin Yutang also wrote that:

"India was the teacher of China in trigonometry, quadratic equations, grammar, phonetics…"

The Egyptians did not have a numerical system suitable for large calculations. For the number 986, they had to use 23 symbols. After the Greeks, the Romans also wanted a system of numbers for mathematical calculations. Indeed, the mathematical systems of the Egyptians, Babylonians, Romans, and even the Chinese were all using independent symbols until they received help from the Indian numeral system. Afterward, it came to be known as Arabic numerals, and eventually, they got what they needed.

One of the greatest mathematicians in the world from France, Pierre Laplace, wrote:

"It is India that gave us the great method of expressing all numbers by means of ten symbols, each receiving a value of position as well as an absolute value. This is an achievement that should be appreciated. The Indians invented the numerical figures used throughout the civilized world. India was the most civilized country of that time in mathematics."

An example is the recent evidence of geometric drafting tools dating back to 2500 BCE found in the Indus Valley. The weights, measures, and decimal division scales obtained from that early period are still quite precise.

Even Professor Monier Williams says in his Indian Wisdom (page 185):

"The invention of algebra and geometry, and their application to astronomy, are to be credited to the Hindus."

The ancient Indians had successfully expressed any number using just ten symbols. These numerals gradually reached the West via North Arabia and Egypt, and by the 11th century, they had reached Europe. Europeans called them Arabic numerals. However, the Arabs themselves called them Hindu numerals (Al-Arkan, Al-Hindu).

The Vedic system also invented zero, which is considered one of the greatest developments in the history of mathematics. The oldest European book on mathematics, known as Codex Vigilanus, can be found in the museum in Madrid. It states:

"From the numerical symbols (digits), we experience that the ancient Hindus had very sharp minds, and other countries were far behind them in counting, geometry, and other sciences. This is proven by their nine digits, with the help of which any number can be written."

Albert

Sanskrit Language

Undoubtedly, the greatest contribution of Vedic culture is the script and language of Sanskrit. Sanskrit is the language of ancient India and Vedic philosophy. It is a perfect language, containing the spiritual vibrations it speaks of.

"Sanskrit language consists of 50 sounds and letters in its alphabet. It has 11,000 roots from which words can be formed. The English language has 500,000 words.

The Sanskrit language has 1700 dhatus (root verbs), 80 upasargas (prefixes), and 20 pratyayas (suffixes). It is believed that Sanskrit has approximately 74,000,000 words. In fact, by using these rules and combining prefixes and suffixes, Sanskrit can provide an infinite number of words whose meanings are entirely determined by grammatical processes.

Bengali, Gurmukhi, Gujarati, Marathi, Odia, and 38 Hindi languages are derived from Sanskrit. The southern languages have been influenced by Sanskrit. Washoe County, Nevada (USA) declared January 12, 2008, as Sanskrit Day.

Words are found in almost all languages like Greek, French, English, Arabic, Urdu, Persian, Indian, Mayan, Slavic, Russian, but only Sanskrit has a distinct identity for each word.

The editor of seven volumes of Indian Antiquities, mentions in Volume IV that the first European Sanskrit scholar, Halhed, said, "It seems that Sanskrit was the original language of the earth."

A.L. Basham, former professor of Asian Civilization at the Australian National University, Canberra, wrote in his book The Wonder That Was India (page 390):

"One of ancient India's greatest achievements is its remarkable alphabet, beginning with the vowels and followed by the consonants, all classified in a very scientific manner."

Astronomy

According to Cassini and Jean-Claude Bailly (1736-93), "According to the true astronomical calculations of the Hindus, the current age of the world, Kali Yuga, began on February 20, 3102 BCE, 2 hours and 27 minutes before the birth of Christ. The Hindu zodiac is the earliest known to man, and the first calendar was made in India around 12,000 BCE." This was stated in Bailly's Histoire de l'Astronomie Ancienne and the proceedings of the Society of Biblical Archaeology, December 1901, Part 1.

Some of the earliest references to Vedic astronomical understanding can be found in texts like the Yajurveda, which states that the Earth remains in space due to the attraction (or gravitational pull) of the Sun. The Atharvaveda also mentions that the Moon depends on the Sun for its light.

Other notable books on astronomy included Vedanga Jyotish, Bhrigu Samhita, and Jyotish Shastra. Indian astronomers were quite knowledgeable about their position. They knew the size of the Earth, the orbits of other planets, the position of the Moon concerning stars, and the phases of the Moon.

Aryabhata, in his Aryabhatiya, also provides valuable information:
- The lunar cycle is 27.322 days, while modern calculation is also 27.322 days.
- He found the Martian year to be 1.881 years, which modern calculations agree with.
- Aryabhata's calculation for Jupiter's period was 11.861 years, close to the modern value of 11.862 years.
- The solar year is 29.477 years, according to Aryabhata, while modern calculation is 29.458 years.

Nineteenth-century French astronomer Jean-Sylvain Bailly was also impressed with the accuracy of the astronomical tables made by ancient Hindus. He said, "…the motions of the stars calculated by the Hindus before 4500 years vary not even a single minute from the tables of Cassini and Meyer (used in Europe in the nineteenth century)." The attracting power of the Sun (due to its gravitational pull) and this is further described in books like the Vishnu Purana, "Indeed, it is neither the rise nor the setting of the Sun; it is ever-present, and these terms (rise and set) merely indicate its appearance and disappearance."

Plastic Surgery

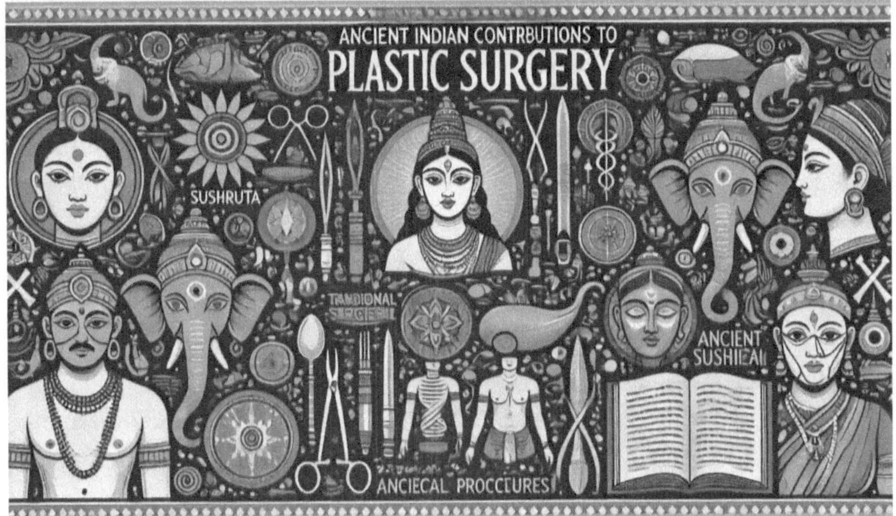

Regarding surgery, known as plastic surgery, it was known in India many years ago. One notable example was observed by two British doctors, Dr. Thomas Crasso and Dr. James Findley. This was in 1793 when a Marathi coachman named Kavasji had to have a new nose. The doctors observed this procedure and presented a report with pictures in the Madras Gazette, which was republished in the October 1794 edition. This report caused a stir in the European medical world at that time.

The entire process of replacing the nose, along with more than 300 other surgical operations, was described in the Sushruta Samhita. Surgeons across Europe studied the above procedure, and after understanding the method, a 30-year-old surgeon named Dr. J.C. Carpue performed a nose transplant on a man in 1814. This operation was also successful. This revolutionized surgical treatment and was named "plastic surgery." All surgeons, including

Dr. Carpue, undoubtedly agreed that plastic surgery is an ancient Indian contribution.

The process of vaccination (creating a vaccine by collecting pus) was performed in India many years before Dr. Jenner, who is said to have discovered vaccination in 1798. The entire process was detailed in an article titled An Account of the Diseases of Bengal; Calcutta, February 10, 1731.

As noted by B.B. Chaube in Science and Technology in Ancient India, "Modern scientists would be very surprised to learn that, besides many sciences, the development of embryology is also credited to India in the Vedic period." There are several references among the Brahmins about the process of knowing how male and female children are born, and ritualistic instructions or guidelines are given (which describe how to conceive a male or female).

Vedanga literature also provides substantial material in this regard. The Puranas, especially the Garuda Purana [along with others], detail how a male is manifested in the womb.

Sushruta Samhita (Sharirasthana, Chapter 5, Paragraph 6) describes the body as follows:

"The body consists of 7 layers of skin, 7 tissues, 7 vessels, 7 elements, 700 tubular vessels, 500 muscles, 900 nerves, 300 bones, 210 joints, 107 vital organs, 24 (blood) vessels, 3 humors, 3 impurities, a collection of 9 sensory organs, 16 tendons, 16 plexuses, 6 muscle bundles, 4 muscle cords, 7 (fibrous) sutures, 14 bone complexes, 14 terminal formations, 22 capillaries, and 2 intestines." Few books of that era provide such detailed descriptions. How these develop in the body is also explained in Sushruta Samhita, presenting a rare explanation.

If ancient India was known for its advancements in medicine and surgery, it also developed means of progress in dentistry.

Dr. Arthur Selwyn-Brown writes in The Physicians Through the Ages (page 274): "You will be surprised to know that dentistry in all its branches was well-known and practiced by ancient Hindu doctors. Exploring Ayurveda, one finds an entire chapter dedicated to the oral cavity, describing all the operations known to modern Western dentistry. After the early development of medicine in early India, it began to spread elsewhere and gained the most popularity in Tibet.

In the 8th century, a major work in four parts, known as Chatush Tantra in Tibetan, titled Amrita Hridaya, was translated from Sanskrit to Tibetan.

The teachings within were attributed to Buddha Bhaisajyaguru. However, some sections are clearly quotations from the Charaka or Sushruta Samhita. Subsequently, this work reached Mongolia and then Russia in the following centuries.

Textile

Will Durant states, "Cotton cultivation in India appears earlier than anywhere else, with its use in fabric at Mohenjo-daro." Dr. Stanley Wolpert, a professor of history at UCLA, writes in his publication India, "Ancient Indians were the first to spin cotton into fabric, providing us with the most comfortable attire for summer."

The spread of cotton to England can be described as follows: In the first century, Arab traders brought fine muslin and calico fabrics from India and sold them in Italy and Spain. Medieval Arabs adopted the textile art from India, and their word qutn gave rise to the English word cotton. The word qutn is derived from the original Sanskrit word "kataan," meaning to spin thread from a cotton ball.

The spinning wheel, or charkha, was possibly invented in India, although its origin is not clear. It reached Europe through the Middle East during the Middle Ages. Professor D.P. Singhal from Queensland University, Australia, provides further clarity in his book India and World Civilization (page 176), stating: "The charkha is an Indian invention."

In ancient India, at least 4000 to 5000 years ago, cotton was cultivated, spun into thread, and woven into fabric. The Greeks were unaware of cotton until Alexander the Great's conquest of India, where they first encountered cotton. They did not find it in Egypt, Mesopotamia, or Persia, the regions they had previously traveled through. Before this, Greeks used only wool in their woven fabrics.

When the French traveler and trader Tavernier visited India in the 17th century, he described the cotton fabrics, stating, "They are so light and beautiful that you can hardly feel them in your hands, and the delicate embroidery is barely visible." In another instance, he writes, "A Persian ambassador returned from India and presented his sultan with a coconut as a gift. The courtiers were astonished by this small gift. But even more astonishing was that when the coconut was opened, it contained a 30-yard roll of [Dacca] muslin fabric."

The famous dye for various shades of blue was extracted from the Indigofera tinctoria plant. By the early 20th century, indigo cultivation covered 1.6 million acres of land in India. Germany began producing this dye on a commercial scale from cheap industrial raw materials in 1897, monopolizing the world market and practically destroying the Indian indigo industry.

It is interesting to note that the Romans were great admirers of Indian textiles, to the extent that much of Rome's gold was taken from its treasure chests to purchase Indian textiles. Some of these early Roman gold coins have been found in various parts of southern India.

Metallurgy

India has a great history of working with metals, smelting, and obtaining alloys, which dates back to 3000 BCE. It is indicated that the first steel weapons for the Mediterranean people came from India.

There are 44 ancient texts describing the process of Indian metallurgy. One of the most famous texts is Rasaratna Samuccaya. It provides details on many aspects of this technology, including the laboratory, crucible furnace, chemical storage vessels, distillation apparatus, and other equipment used in the laboratory.

According to Will Durant, "The Hindus were the first people to mine gold. Greek visitors like Megasthenes mentioned this in their records. Most of the gold used in the Persian Empire in the 5th century BCE came from India. India also mined silver, copper, zinc, lead, tin, and iron."

Steel Making

Another early development of ancient India was the ability of its artisans to produce high-quality steel. S. Ramachandran, in his book The Steel of India, writes:

"Steel was known in ancient India from ancient times and was referred to as Ayas in the Vedas. Archaeological evidence has shown that ancient Indians knew the art of making steel."

As noted by Ferguson in his book A History of Indian and Eastern Architecture, "The Iron Pillar of Delhi opens our eyes to the fact that the Hindus were capable of making and welding iron pillars larger than any known to the rest of the world and later copied in Europe. It is almost a marvel that, despite being exposed to wind and rain for centuries, it has not rusted and the inscriptions are still very clear…"

Copper was another metal that ancient Indians learned to use proficiently. As early as 2000 BCE, people were molding copper into fine-edged tools and axes.

Bronze was known in the Indus Valley region before 3000 BCE. Bronze objects were made using the lost-wax casting technique, which is still used today.

Mentions of zinc technology in Greek texts indicate that zinc items were traded from India as early as the 6th or 5th century BCE.

Charaka mentioned gold and silver needles as essential items in the lying-in room. He also suggested gold, silver, or iron knives for cutting the umbilical cord of newborns. In Manusmriti, a ceremony is performed at the birth of a boy, where the newborn is given a mixture of honey and ghee on a golden spoon for tasting.

Tempering steel to perfection was unknown to Europe but brought to completion in India. Alexander received a priceless gift of steel, not 30 pounds of gold, from the Indian king.

India led in many chemical and pharmaceutical industries, including dyeing, tanning, soap making, glass and pottery, cement, and metallurgy. Indians were far ahead of European experts in many techniques. The secret of making Damascus steel was learned by the Arabs from the Persians, who had taken it from India.

The sandalwood tree was native to India. It was grown in Karnataka and used for its aromatic properties, making it a fine product for export to Greece, Arabia, and other places. Musk, another aromatic substance, was collected from the gland of the male musk deer and became highly sought after. Camphor was another fragrant item exported from India since ancient times, often used in rituals and prayers.

Vedic culture also utilized diamonds and many other precious and semi-precious stones. However, this science was not just about knowing the value of the gems and how to use them for adornment, but also about using them in astrology to counteract the negative effects of planets or even enhance their positive powers. Garuda Purana and Agni Purana contain much information of this type.

Agricultural Development

Agriculture has always been an essential occupation in India. In the Rigveda and Atharvaveda, agriculture is considered a great profession.

India was one of the oldest regions for plant cultivation, including rice, jute, cotton, pulses, black pepper, wheat, rye, flax, walnuts, apples, pears, and mangoes. Archaeological findings have revealed that many species of winter cereals, such as barley, oats, and wheat, along with legumes like lentils and chickpeas, were grown in northwest India before the 6th millennium BCE.

The Atharvaveda divides plants into seven subcategories, such as trees, grasses, herbs for medicine, shrubs, creepers, etc. References to these can also be found in texts like the Mahabharata, Vishnu Purana, and Matsya Purana.

Sage Charaka mentions that trees have life and emotions similar to other living beings. The texts provide a list of tools, methods for better agricultural management for higher crop yields, tools used, operations, harvesting, dealing with rainfall, managing cattle, as well as advice on seed collection and storage.

Krishi-Parashara and Brihat Samhita are known for providing simple astrological models to predict rainfall using basic astrology based on seasonal climatic conditions. For example, Parashara's method used the position of the moon and sun, while Varahamihira's Brihat Samhita (505-587 BCE) considered the position of the lunar phases. These methods are still used by many farmers.

The Rigveda includes procedures for maintaining cows and managing them with proper food or forage and water to drink.

Vrksayurveda Parashara, authored by Sage Parashara, provides advanced botanical knowledge in six parts. Sage Parashara deeply understood the entire process of plant growth, development, and care. Vrksayurveda Parashara provides a detailed description of the process of a seed growing into a tree. This indicates that the discovery of life in plants by Sir J.C. Bose was not an original discovery but rather a confirmation of what the Vedas and ancient India already knew. In fact, this is also confirmed in the Rigveda (10.97.21) and the Mahabharata (Shanti Parva, Chapter 184). These books suggest practical methods for good farming while conserving the world's resources and environment. Farmers of that time were already using crop rotation to enhance soil fertility, and row planting was known since ancient times.

We also find that the Garuda Purana and Agni Purana provide instructions on dealing with animal disorders and livestock management. Ayurveda has a separate section called Shalihotra Samhita, which is crucial for the treatment of horses. According to some veterinarians, this book is better than modern books on horse treatment.

For instance, in the western desert of Rajasthan, in Jaisalmer, the central fort's king's palace was built in such a way that every drop of water falling into it was collected and stored for later use. Pathways were made to collect the breeze from the air so that a cooling effect could be felt in every part of the palace.

The Vishnu Purana and Srimad Bhagavatam also describe the importance of establishing wells and water tanks. But once built, the care of these wells and tanks was taken by the rulers of the state or region. Rice cultivation cannot be done without ample water, for which irrigation is one of the main necessities. With the development of irrigation in ancient India, it became a place where rice could be easily grown.

Art and Music

Music has been known and understood in India since ancient times, and it formed the primary basis of the Samaveda for chanting mantras. The knowledge of music and the number of ragas and raginis is vast.

The main Indian musical instruments included Sarod, Veena, Sarangi, Tambura, Harmonium, Ghatam, Tabla, and Sitar. These instruments were not simple; they required special materials, craftsmanship, and processes, along with years of rigorous practice to master them.

By the time of the Yajurveda, various types of professional musicians had emerged, such as flutists, drummers, and conch blowers.

Thus, the cultivation of music by Indians began at a very early age, as seen with the names of the seven notes (in order) - Sa (Shadja), Re (Rishabha), Ga (Gandhara), Ma (Madhyama), Pa (Panchama), Dha (Dhaivata), Ni (Nishada), appearing in the Samaveda and in their current sequence.

Saptak means that the eighth note is the same as the first note of the octave but at a higher level. The Indian saptak (seven notes) and the Western octave are as follows:

- Indian Saptak: Sa, Re, Ga, Ma, Pa, Dha, Ni, Sa
- Western Octave: Do, Re, Mi, Fa, Sol, La, Ti, Do

In Indian tradition, literature and music are inseparable. Various ragas and raginis are designated for different times of the day or seasons of the year to evoke specific moods and emotions.

Six major ragas include:

- Basant: Brings the sweetness and freshness of spring to the listeners' minds.
- Shree Raga: Conveys the peace and calm of the evening.
- Megh Malhar: Evokes the mood of an impending storm and rain.
- Deepak: Called to light the lamps of approaching death, or even to burn the singer's body in flames, causing him to die (no wonder it is hardly known now).
- Bhairav: Very popular and reminiscent of the effects of the coming morning, the freshness of a new day, and the singing of birds.
- Malkauns: Creates a sense of activity.

Under the Muhammadans, Hindu music began to fade. Thus, dance and music came to a standstill as they were banned by Muslims. However, to save themselves, many Hindu musicians converted to Islam.

Therefore, we find the common knowledge that most Muslims in India are of Hindu or familial descent. Thus, many Islamic musicians have emerged from the Vedic system of music.

Vedic Dance

Like art, dance in India was not merely an expression of an artist's emotional mindset or imagination but an interpretation of higher spiritual principles. In fact, among Vedic deities, Lord Shiva is known as Nataraja, the king of dancers. His dance is based on the rhythm of energy spread across the universe and the destruction of illusory (imaginary) energy, which offers all souls the opportunity to attain liberation (moksha) by being freed from illusion.

Bharata Muni wrote his Natya Shastra, in which he explained that it was Lord Brahma, the secondary engineer of universal creation, who brought dance (natya) and drama to the people of Earth millions of years ago, soon after the Earth's creation. Ranjani Sehgal explains how this might have happened: "Once, the gods requested Lord Brahma to create another Veda that would be easy for the common man to understand, which is especially important in the Kali Yuga. Fulfilling their wish, Lord Brahma composed the Pancham-Veda, the fifth Veda, or Natya Veda.

Brahma took pathya (words) from the Rigveda, abhinaya (body movements, gestures) from the Yajurveda, geet (music and chants) from the Samaveda, and rasa (emotions and emotional expressions) from the Atharvaveda to create the fifth Veda, Natya Veda. After composing this Veda, Lord Brahma handed it over to Sage Bharata and asked him to spread it on Earth. Following this, Sage Bharata concentrated on the Natya Shastra. Bharata, along with groups of Gandharvas (celestial musicians) and Apsaras (celestial dancing girls), performed natya and dance before Lord Shiva. It is also possible that the term Bharatanatyam was partially named after Sage Bharata.

The walls of the temples in Chidambaram, South India, depict 108 postures. Many dance techniques have been derived from the Natya Shastra, such as Bharatanatyam, Kuchipudi, Kathak, Kathakali, Odissi, Mohiniattam, Krishna Attam, Bhagavata Mela, Manipuri, etc. These have also developed in various ways of telling stories based on epics like the Mahabharata, Ramayana, or stories from the Panchatantra, Hitopadesha, or Krishna Leela from the Bhagavata Purana, or other Puranas.

Ancient Indian classical dance was highly influential. Today, this ancient art of Indian dance is enjoyed by wide audiences and holds a significant place on the international stage. In the Vedic tradition, art was never merely a representation of an artist's imagination. It was always a beautiful way to express truth and principles, levels of reality that might exist beyond our sense of judgment. It was always pure and true.

In ancient times, art and painting provided spiritual energy. Thus, a painting or symbol became a gateway to spiritual essence. The meaning of darshan is not only to see the deity but also to enter into the exchange of seeing and being seen by the deity.

British researcher Mr. Griffith says, "The artists who painted the Ajanta murals were supreme in the world of creation. Even the straight upright lines drawn with simple brush strokes on the walls of Ajanta are astonishing."

Knowledge of Sea Routes

The Rigveda (1.25.7) describes how Varuna had complete knowledge of all the sea routes followed by ships. In Rigveda (2.48.3), it is mentioned that Indian merchants also sent ships for foreign trade.

Epics like the Ramayana and Mahabharata mention ships and sea travel, and the Puranas such as Matsya, Varaha, and Markandeya Puranas also contain stories of sea voyages. In the Kishkindha Kanda of the Ramayana, Sugriva instructs the monkey leaders to search for Sita in the cities and mountains located on the islands across the sea. The Ramayana also describes how merchants traveled across the seas and brought gifts for kings.

In the Mahabharata, it is described how the sons of Draupadi provided protection to their uncles by providing chariots. Another passage mentions how the Pandavas escaped from a planned destruction with the help of a specially constructed ship. This ship was large, equipped with machinery and all kinds of weapons for war, and capable of facing storms and waves.

The Brihat Samhita by Varahamihira in the 5th century and the Sanskrit text Yukti Kalpataru by the 11th-century king Bhoja provide information about the classification, size, and materials used in the construction of ships. These texts also detail how to equip ships for passengers' comfort, or for transporting goods, animals, or royal artifacts. There were three different sizes of ships: Sarvamandira, Madhyamamandira, and Agramandira.

Ancient Indians traveled to various parts of the world not only for trade purposes but also to spread their culture. Thus, Vedic influence spread worldwide. It appears that trade with countries like Egypt was conducted around 2540 BCE from that port.

In 1292 CE, when Marco Polo visited India, he described Indian ships as "made of cedar wood, covered with boards, and sealed with iron nails." The cracks were filled with a special type of glue. These ships were so large that they required around 300 sailors to operate. They had many small rooms for people to live in, with every kind of comfort provided in these rooms. When the bottom or base started to wear out, a new layer was added on top. Sometimes, a ship had up to six layers, one on top of the other.

Another traveler, Nicolo Conti, who visited India in the 15th century, wrote: "Indian ships are much larger than ours. Their base is made with three planks to withstand storms. Some ships are constructed in such a way that if one part becomes useless, the rest of the ship remains functional."

Another traveler to India, named Bertham, writes: "The wooden planks are joined so tightly that not a drop of water can pass through. Anchors were sometimes made from heavy stones. It would take a ship eight days to travel from Iran to Cape Comorin (Kanyakumari)."

Vasco da Gama mentions in his diaries, available in the British Museum, that when his ship arrived near Zanzibar in Africa, he saw a ship three times the size of his own. He met the owner of the ship, a Gujarati merchant named Chandan, who brought cedar wood and teak from India along with spices, and took diamonds back to the port of Cochin. When Vasco da Gama met him, Chandan was dressed in simple clothes. When the merchant asked Vasco where he was headed, he said he was going to explore India. So, Vasco da Gama followed him to India.

Further evidence shows that ancient India was a leader in global trade relations with people like the Phoenicians, Jews, Assyrians, Greeks, and

Romans in ancient times, and with Egyptians, Romans, Turks, Portuguese, Dutch, and English more recently. Papers presented at a conference on maritime travel in Delhi in 1994 show that Indian cotton was exported to South and Central America around 2500 BCE. Another report suggests that Indian cotton reached Mexico by 4000 BCE, during the Rigvedic period.

The simple fact is that India's maritime history predates the birth of Western civilization. It is believed that the world's first tidal dock was built around 2300 BCE during the Harappan civilization at Lothal, near the present-day port of Mangrol on the Gujarat coast. From the second millennium BCE, Kerala had maritime trade with many countries in West Asia and Eastern Europe. Additionally, Indian ships traded with other countries in the Pacific and Indian Oceans.

The Roman writer Pliny mentions that Indian merchants took large quantities of gold from Rome in exchange for precious stones, skins, clothes, spices, sandalwood, perfumes, herbs, silk, cotton, and other Indian products. The estimated daily revenue from Western regions between 844-848 CE was 200 man (eight tons) of gold.

How the British Destroyed India's Maritime Industry

The decline of Indian maritime power began in the 13th century and by the time the Portuguese arrived in India, Indian maritime power had almost vanished. Later, they introduced a system of licenses and permits for trade.

By the 17th century, European ships were a maximum of 600 tons. However, in India, they saw large ships like the Ghogha, which were over 1500 tons. When Westerners encountered these Indian ships, they were amazed.

European companies began using these ships and opened several new factories to build ships using Indian artisans. In 1811, Lieutenant Walker wrote, "English ships needed repairs every 12th year. But Indian ships made of teak worked for more than 50 years without any repairs." The East India Company had a ship named Darya Daulat, which ran for 87 years without any repairs.

French traveler Walter Salvins wrote in his book Les Hindous in 1811, "The Hindus were always ahead in shipbuilding, and even today, they can teach Europeans a thing or two. The English, who were good at learning the art, learned many things about shipbuilding from the Hindus."

British shipping companies could not tolerate the Indian art of shipbuilding and began pressuring the East India Company not to use Indian ships. In 1811, Colonel Walker provided data to prove that building Indian ships was much cheaper. If only Indian ships were included in the British fleet, there would be great savings. This worried British shipbuilders and traders.

London dock workers were the first to raise the issue, saying, "All our work will be finished."

The East India Company Board of Directors wrote that "the fear and respect that Indian sailors had for European conduct disappeared when they saw our social life upon coming here. When they return to their country, they will spread bad things about us among the Asians, and we will lose our superiority, which will be harmful."

In response, the British Parliament formed a committee headed by Sir Robert Peel. In 1814, a law was passed according to which Indians lost the right to become British sailors, and it became mandatory to employ at least three-quarters British sailors on British ships. Ships not owned by a Briton were not allowed to enter the port of London, and a rule was made that only ships built by the British in England could bring goods to England. This was strictly followed from 1863 onwards. Taxes on goods brought by Indian ships were increased, and efforts were made to exclude them from trade. This is the story of the destruction of the Indian art of shipbuilding.

Trade between ancient India and other countries was conducted not only through maritime capabilities but also through land routes extending to China, Turkistan, Persia, Babylon, Egypt, Greece, and Rome, which continued further.

Today, India is still very advanced in the shipbuilding business, primarily in small and medium-sized ships. The English word navigation actually comes from the Sanskrit word navigati.

Education in Ancient India

India's early education system was village-based. It was the local sages (rishis) and Brahmins who taught qualified local students. The place of education was called a gurukul or the guru's place. The sage teacher was like a father to the students. The primary aim of the school was to transform young students into capable individuals well-versed in the principles of Vedic Dharma, which are the foundations of being honorable and respected.

The objective was to foster the physical, moral, intellectual, and spiritual development of the students, along with building their character so they could live peacefully in the world. Such a sophisticated education system was rarely found elsewhere.

The main subject was Atmavidya (knowledge of the self), after which all other subjects could be easily studied. These included sciences, arts and crafts, music, mathematics (such as geometry and algebra), astronomy or astrology, logic, history, poetry, grammar, and Vedic scriptures. Many schools also trained soldiers in the use of weapons and in training horses and elephants.

The methods of imparting knowledge included teaching and lecturing, recitation, dialogue, and then self-study. The Vedas, ancient education, were further developed under the guidance of the Upanishads, which made it more advanced.

Moreover, such education focused on character building, learning good habits, following a proper daily routine by waking up early, performing daily rituals, and, of course, speaking the truth and living a simple life. For many years, this tradition was based on oral teachings rather than written words. Education was provided not just through memorization but through realization, and sound had its significance in generating the energy of the knowledge described in the vibrations of words.

In this way, students were given oral lessons, which they reflected upon, studied, learned, and memorized. In the Vedic tradition, knowledge could be provided or received through three basic stages: Shravan (hearing), Manan (contemplation), and Nididhyasan (realization).

The goal was to provide real education and culture for the development of all humanity. Students, in return for free education, would fulfill duties towards the teacher. This could include helping maintain and clean the ashram, assisting in grazing cows, or helping in rituals. However, the primary duty of the student was to study and learn.

Vedic education was free for everyone (regardless of caste and religion).

After completing their education, the guru or teacher would give final instructions: "Always speak the truth, perform your duties. Do not break the old traditions after giving your teacher the final offering. Never abandon Dharma. Do not miss the opportunity to become great. Consider your mother a goddess, your father a god. Treat your teacher (acharya) as a god. Treat guests (atithi) as gods. Perform good deeds. Whatever gifts you give, give them with full love and respect."

"If any doubt arises in your mind regarding Dharma or righteousness, seek advice from the Brahmins who are superior and tender-hearted, and act as they say. This is my instruction to you, follow it."

Justice M. Rama Jois, retired Chief Justice of the Punjab and Haryana High Court, said to the author in 2010, "This was indeed the best way to rid the country of all the corruption we see." He mentioned that during pre-independence times, children would hear about examples of Dharma from great epics like the Mahabharata and Ramayana or Puranas and about the great heroes who acted under the rules of Dharma in various situations. Thus, children were educated about proper character and how to act as proper humans even before learning to read and write. They were taught to discern what is right and wrong in different situations of life.

Unfortunately, this changed after 1947 when the new administration of independent India decided that learning the principles of Dharma was religious study, and the new government could no longer support such preschools. Thus, all such principles under Dharma were no longer taught in Indian schools.

As M. Rama Jois pointed out in his book Dharma: The Global Ethic, "All our current problems are the direct result of disagreeing with education on Dharma under the influence of materialistic education. There is no alternative to Dharma. It is the eternal truth."

The Mahabharata (Shanti Parva, 90.3) also says that "the proper duty of a king or any ruler or politician is to govern according to Dharma and not to enjoy the luxuries of life." Thus, a politician is supposed to follow his duties with the benefit of the people in mind under the guidance of the rules of Dharma, not for personal gain.

The basic rules of Dharma as stated in the Manu Smriti (10.63) are:
- Ahimsa (non-violence),
- Satya (truth),
- Asteya (not acquiring illicit wealth),
- Shaucham (purity), and
- Indriya Nigraha (control over senses).

When such training is received at a young age, it can last a lifetime. The principles of Dharma are not regional or religious training but are secular training. Religion often divides, while Dharma unites by seeing everyone equally. Dharma can be applied to all humans. Thus, it maintains harmony in society and does not create conflict.

It is said that the Nalanda University had numerous students and teachers. Initially built in a small village, it developed into a flourishing city and center of Buddhist teaching. Lord Buddha gave many lectures here in the Pravarika forest and Rajgir. It was known for teaching Vedanta, Samkhya, and Jyotish.

Due to some religious conflicts, other communities tried to destroy as many Vedic books as possible to make Indians less attracted to and less trusting of their own culture.

Vedic Economics

The ancient Indian economy was primarily a local, village-based economy. The first principle of Vedic understanding is to view everything as the energy of the supreme power.

Conducting business in a way that intentionally deceives others hardens our hearts and thoughts, making us unable to discover the divine beauty in all living beings and even within ourselves. Business should be conducted with honesty, and ancient India followed this type of business ethics. Quick profits earned through dishonesty and fraud will undoubtedly bring us down. Business must be based on religious principles.

Nowadays, we have seen companies with the power and motive to earn massive profits producing various foods, medicines, beverages, etc., claiming they are highly beneficial to health without any side effects. Over time, we have learned that such products have indeed been imposed on the public, causing harmful side effects. However, we must always remember that a story presented as a fact by a company whose motive is power, control, or profit is usually a story that should not be trusted.

Ancient India, during the Vedic era, completely avoided such practices. Villages and towns and their local economy would develop when there was an abundance of grains, vegetables, herbs, fruit-bearing trees, rivers flowing with fresh and clean water, and hills rich in minerals. In this scenario, there would be plenty for everyone.

If society has sufficient natural resources in this way, why should it opt for vast industrial complexes that require the labor of men sent to dark factories, where they spend their lives for a dollar, and then have to give a portion of their earnings to government taxes?

The more society depends on artificial needs, the more insecure it becomes. Thus, whenever there is a fear of not having enough oil, gas, electricity, or when the prices of such modern commodities become too high, civilization suffers, and the economy slows down. We have now become so dependent on them that we feel we cannot survive without them. As a result, people are forced to struggle to buy more material things and earn more money. In this way, they are tied to a system whose goal is profit rather than providing real benefits to society or living in a balanced economy.

Today's economic system keeps you controlled, busy with the bills you pay. You are forced into a system where you work for the almighty dollar to pay for the basic needs of life. Often, you are forced to work for others' benefit in the business or industry that hires you.

Even if you are your own boss or a professional like a doctor or lawyer, you must obtain a license and work within the system with the fear of losing your license.

In other words, your time to think about higher philosophical thoughts, self-development, or spiritual practice is limited because you must ensure that you have the money to pay for everything you need in today's life.

Many people are so afraid that they cannot change their jobs (even if they don't like them) just because the job allows them to pay all their bills and maintain some balance in their lives. This is the nature of today's economic system for most people.

This is why many people today have to work two or three jobs. Such a lifestyle causes a lot of stress, and some people start behaving despairingly, leading to increased crime. It keeps people away from their spiritual potential and social development, making society godless and disorganized. This is not the purpose of human existence at all.

The Vedic system was to free people from this cycle of working for unnecessary needs. It aimed to free you to work for your basic needs while keeping time and energy for your spiritual and social development.

According to the Vedic economic system, the fundamental principle of economic development is land and its produce. Whoever controls the land controls the food. Whoever controls the food and fuel controls the world. Therefore, the land should always be in the hands of local farmers so that everything is shared, and all people can develop.

In conclusion, we must understand that the greatest form of pollution in this world is competition for position, power, and wealth. It is natural to work for better ways of doing business and producing higher quality products. Whoever has the best will succeed. But competition based on envy, jealousy, and power, or just for more money, forces individuals and companies to accept wrong ways to move forward, gain more market share, get more customers, and produce cheaper products. To cleanse this world of the ruling ship of money, dirty politics, and false and misleading economy, a new system must rise.

We must be strong enough to make such a change and then use the principles of Vedic Dharma to create a balanced and spiritually developed society.

Military and Martial Arts

The earliest form of military science is described in the standard Vedic text called Dhanurveda. The use and training of weapons were the most important parts of the military, which included the use of bows and arrows while riding horses in those days. It involved not only shooting a single arrow but also shooting multiple arrows at multiple targets. These included Yantramuktas (projectile missiles), Hastamuktas (hand-thrown weapons), Muktamuktas (held and thrown weapons like spears, tridents, or swords), and natural weapons like fists, fingers, and feet.

The Vedic Aryans were well acquainted with the ingredients of gunpowder, such as sulfur, charcoal, and saltpeter, all of which were easily obtained locally. Greek writers described the use of firearms by Hindus. It appears that rockets and cannons were early Indian inventions before they became popular in other regions.

Brahmastra was another weapon frequently mentioned in Vedic scriptures. These were a type of mantra-infused weapons attached to arrows that, upon hitting their target, produced an effect similar to a nuclear explosion, unlike today's nuclear bombs that destroy everything in the area.

India is also known for its unique form of martial arts, which are among the earliest developments that have existed for thousands of years. Many forms of martial arts that emerged from here were first introduced by techniques from India. Some styles of martial arts from India went along with Buddhism to Tibet, then to China, and later to Japan.

In India, martial arts were known as Shastravidya and Dhanurvidya. Texts like the Bhagavata Purana, Vishnu Purana, Mahabharata, and others include descriptions of individual fights and the weapons used, such as trees, swords, bows and arrows, rocks, and fists.

Even dance movements of styles like Kathakali, which is also famous in Kerala, were incorporated into martial arts. Kalaripayattu is a well-known system of martial arts in India, mostly originating from Kerala.

One of the oldest forms of martial arts is Lathi or the long staff. This art has been practiced in India for thousands of years and is still prevalent in many rural areas today. The Lathi was used for self-defense and warfare, and it is still taught in many martial arts schools today.

Aircraft/Aviation in Ancient India

We need to understand that the Vedic concept of universal time is divided into different epochs. For example, a day of Brahma is equivalent to 4,320,000,000 years on Earth. Brahma's night is equally long, and there are 360 such days and nights in a year. Each day of Brahma is divided into one thousand cycles of four epochs, namely Satya Yuga, Treta Yuga, Dvapara Yuga, and finally Kali Yuga.

Satya Yuga lasts for 1,728,000 years and is an age of purity when all inhabitants live very long lives and can fully develop in spiritual understanding, magical abilities, and remarkable powers. These abilities include changing one's size, becoming very large or very small, very heavy or even weightless, acquiring any desirable object, being free from all desires, or even flying in the sky to any place they want. Thus, mechanical flight was not necessary at that time.

As the sequence of ages continued, the purity of people, as well as their magical abilities, decreased by 25% in each subsequent age. The age of Treta Yuga is 1,296,000 years.

Vedic Environmentalism

Some activities to protect the environment, whether through water conservation systems, the development of rivers and canals, and maintaining land and forests through agricultural systems, are recorded in ancient India.

The environment means nature, and whose nature is it? It is the nature of God. Did anyone else create it? In fact, humanity is still trying to explore the complexity of the environment. In all our inventions, most of the materials and resources we use are given by God. And we need to show proper respect for it. Thinking that we own everything is an illusion. The brain with which we think is not made by us but given by God.

Neglecting the environment, misusing our natural resources, not properly managing land and forests, in all ways is disrespectful to God, and we should never waste resources. However, if those who have no real spiritual understanding start to misuse the earth to get whatever they want, then the supply of resources begins to dwindle, and the earth, being a living entity, stops producing or responding to the needs of society as it used to.

Instead of respecting the earth and cooperating in sharing its resources, when we fight over them, it is most disappointing for Mother Earth. Then there will be scarcity, drought, and forest fires; gradually, prices of goods will rise, and more people will become poor, spreading poverty across the world.

The proper vision and Vedic understanding are that everything belongs to the Supreme Lord. We certainly cannot take them with us when we leave this body. The proper way to use anything is to serve God and take care of the environment.

Personal Freedom and Governance as Derived from India

CHAPTER 17

Personal Freedom and Governance as Derived from India

As India's President A.P.J. Abdul Kalam once rightly said: "In our 3000 years of history, people from all over the world have come and ruled us, occupied our lands and minds. Since Alexander, the Greeks, Turks, Mughals, Portuguese, British, French, Dutch, all came and looted and occupied us, yet we have never done this to any other nation. We have not conquered anyone's land or history, nor have we attempted to do so, because we respect others' freedom. This is the freedom that Vedic culture has always promoted.

Even today, India is the seventh-largest and the second-most populous country in the world. With a constitution and a nationally elected parliament, it is the largest democracy.

In this ideology, Dr. Will said, "Let us remember that India was the motherland of our race, and Sanskrit the mother of Europe's languages; she was the mother of philosophy; mother, through the Arabs, of much of our mathematics; mother, through the Buddha, of the ideals embodied in Christianity; mother, through the village community, of self-government and democracy. Mother India is in many ways the mother of us all."

The Vedic civilization had great thinkers who helped originate many additional political ideas. For example, Pandit Kautilya, popularly known as Chanakya, established principles in his Arthashastra that are still used by organizations today, such as NATO (North Atlantic Treaty Organization).

Texts like the Mahabharata contain a wealth of information about government and the duties of a king or ruler. Furthermore, these Vedic principles found in the ancient Mahabharata and other Vedic texts apply to any leader, whether local, state, or national. Any ruler should have a proper constitution that clarifies reality before taking any authoritative position. The purpose of the government and the country's ruler is to protect dharma and all the seekers of truth who follow it.

Principles of Dharma

Dharma refers to the path that helps in bringing and maintaining harmony both personally and socially, and the truth that can free us from negative thoughts and lead us to the ultimate reality.

It is stated that the main objective of a country's constitution should be to protect Dharma and uphold righteousness among the people according to the laws of Dharma.

The constitution should be written only after reviewing Vedic texts that contain the universal standard of spirituality for the development and growth of society.

In Vedic standards, this is called Rama Rajya, as the ruler of that time, Lord Rama, worked for the benefit of all and everyone cooperated together.

In Sanskrit, the chief protector of the people is called Kshatriya. This word means warrior, but primarily, it refers to one who protects people from harm or suffering, or one who removes problems and difficulties.

Protecting all beings is the supreme duty of a proper Kshatriya. Kshatriyas should take up arms only for defense, whether for individuals or the community as a whole. A Kshatriya who does not demonstrate their strength accordingly and avoids acting to their full potential out of fear of losing their life is worthy of being called a thief.

A king who wishes to be great should avoid six faults: sleep, drowsiness, fear, anger, laziness, and procrastination. These six virtues should not be forgotten: truth, charity, compassion, benevolence, forgiveness, and patience.

India - The Home of Greatest Philosophy and Spiritual Culture

In addition to all the developments in science, mathematics, architecture, agriculture, and medicine that came from ancient India, it has also provided the world with the greatest philosophy and spiritual culture adopted by many countries.

The teachings of the soul, God, the system of reincarnation, karma, dharma, and yoga practices offered by India come with great spiritual experiences. These teachings were never imposed on the external world but were shared through deep understanding, logic, and profound knowledge of culture, leading many to study Indian Vedic culture.

Due to some misunderstandings during the British Empire, this treasure and knowledge have been disappearing these days. By re-educating people about Vedic culture and philosophy in India, we can regain this true and pure knowledge.

Many groups have already started teaching about ancient Vedic texts. It is essential for the younger generation to know this.

We still have Vedic texts like the Rigveda, Atharvaveda, Yajurveda, and Samaveda, along with the Brahmanas, Aranyakas, Upanishads, Vedanta Sutras, historical texts like the Ramayana and Mahabharata, which include the Bhagavad Gita and the Puranas.

The great Vedic culture has been mentioned by many great writers and literati of that time. The writer Philip Rawson mentioned in Southeast Asian Art: "India's culture has been one of the most powerful civilizing forces in the world."

Countries in the Far East like China, Korea, Tibet, and Mongolia owe a debt to India for importing inspiring ideas for themselves.

Henry David Thoreau said, "In the morning, I bathe my intellect in the stupendous and cosmogonal philosophy of the Bhagavad Gita." In the history of philosophy, Dr. Enfield says, "We found that Pythagoras had visited India to acquire knowledge, along with Anaxarchus, Pyrrho, and others who later became great philosophers in Greece."

According to the texts of "The Discovery of India" written by Nehru, it seems that as people rediscover the branches of Vedic spiritual philosophy, they will embrace it eagerly once again.

Annie Besant also appreciated Indian culture; she said that epics like the Mahabharata and the Gita are invaluable. In her book, she mentions, "The Hindu lifelines of India, after nearly 40 years of study, I have found nothing so perfect, so philosophical, so spiritual as the great religion of Hinduism. The more you know it, the more you will love it, the more you understand it, the more you will value it."

The truth is that Indians do not appreciate their culture as much as they should. The problem is that Vedic culture has been fading away from India for many generations. Indians show no interest in their own culture. People go to California searching for yoga teachers, but the truth is many foreigners come to India, saving money to get the best yoga teachers.

How India Lost Its Identity

Many people wonder why India lost its identity despite its vast contributions to the world. During the colonization of India, there was a systematic effort by the British to dismantle traditional systems and knowledge. This trend continued even after independence.

Furthermore, there was a group of scholars interested in converting Hindus to Christianity by any means necessary.

According to Sir Monier Williams, a professor of Sanskrit at Oxford University, a foundation's purpose was to translate religious texts written in Sanskrit so that they could easily communicate with the locals of India.

The second agenda was the education system introduced by the British.

T.B. Macaulay aimed to convert as many Hindus to Christianity as possible so that Indians could cooperate more effectively with British (English) administration.

For this purpose, Macaulay wrote to his father in 1836, while serving as the chairman of the Board of Education in India:

"Our English schools are flourishing wonderfully. If our education plans are followed, there will not be a single idolater left among the respectable classes in Bengal; I heartily rejoice in this project. The Sanskrit language is not of so much importance as English."

"We must do our best to form a class who may be interpreters between us and the millions whom we govern, a class of persons, Indian in blood and color, but English in taste, in opinions, in morals, and in intellect."

Macaulay was not in favor of the current administration as he wanted to develop his own English class with limited means so that all people could get accustomed to this English culture.

Macaulay's plan was to eradicate India's Vedic culture and make the people of India forget all its advancements, science, and technology, and contributions to world progress; and the British system succeeded in this plan.

This is why Indians have been unable to regain their status and high development.

Do not forget that the achievements that have brought glory to India still include Indians today. Even today, Indian students are among the most talented in the world.

The author has observed that most of the top students in American classrooms are from India.

India can be progressive as it was before. Corruption is widespread, and we can only overcome it by adhering to its eradication.

Agriculture

The global agricultural trade is worth $4 trillion.

Until the 18th century, 83% of India was engaged in farming. By the 19th century, this reduced to 70%. By 1970, it had decreased to 43%, and by 2024, it is only 15%. In the 18th century, we exported 33% of the world's food grains, which has now dwindled to just 0.3%. In the 18th century, there was no poverty.

Currently, about 500 million people in India are unemployed.

In the 18th century, we used organic seeds and organic fertilizers to produce nutritious crops, which saved on chemical and fertilizer costs, and people were healthy and prosperous.

Today, India's annual expenditure on chemicals and fertilizers is ₹60,000 crores, and ₹120 billion on medicines.

Indonesia stopped farming, and today, the value of one dollar is equivalent to 16,500 Indonesian currency. Currently, one dollar is equivalent to ₹80 in India. If we also stop farming, it won't take long for us to become like Indonesia.

If we do not save farming, the country will not survive. For the welfare of human civilization worldwide, the entire country must adopt organic farming and organic fertilizers.

The Bill & Melinda Gates Foundation and the Rockefeller Foundation have created a seed bank called Seed Vault, which has collected around 4.5 million organic seeds from around the world.

Genetically Modified Organisms (GMOs) mean organisms whose characteristics have been changed, usually by making one or more alterations to the genome using high-tech genetic engineering. GMOs fall under biotechnology. To create GMOs, the desired genes from one organism's DNA are targeted and added to another organism.

GMOs and Monsanto's dominance in the global food seed market have led to a form of dictatorship. Initially, they began selling chemicals and fertilizers globally under the name of the Green Revolution, which resulted in severe agricultural damage worldwide, rendering millions of hectares of land barren and forcing farmers into unemployment and suicide.

GMO companies are banned in 39 countries, but in India, 90% of the agricultural market is still dominated by GMOs. For example, hybrid seeds for wheat, rice, cotton, etc., are sold by GMO companies.

Practical Solutions for Soil Health and Farmer Welfare

1. Compliance with Current Laws: Agricultural recommendations by institutions should comply with existing food laws.
2. National Heritage of Soil Fertility: Soil fertility should be declared a national asset or heritage, with agricultural departments responsible for its maintenance. Despite claims of increased production by chemical industries, soil fertility worldwide has declined.
3. Shift from Irrigation to Moisturization: To conserve soil, crops, crop nutrient value, energy, and water, the term "irrigation" should be replaced with "moisturization."
4. Redefining Yield: The term "yield" needs definition. Is it just gross weight, or should it also relate to nutritional value, compliance with food laws, and food quality?

5. Clarifying Fertilizer: The term "fertilizer" needs clear definition, distinguishing between boosters and authentic fertilizers.

6. Teaching Vedic Agriculture: We need to start teaching Vedic agriculture, including subjects like Vrikshayurveda, Agnihotra, Panchang, Prakash Nighantu, etc.

7. Stop Subsidies: Subsidies degrade the farmer's dignity and make them dependent. Instead of subsidies, farmers should be given fair prices, including cost price and profit. End the exploitation of farmers. Let's return to our culture and promote it globally. With the current system, we can never achieve sustainability.

To achieve sustainability, our entire socio-economic structure needs to shift to Vedic methods, especially in agriculture!

Indian Medicine

The whole world knows that when a pandemic like COVID-19 struck, people turned to traditional medical practices for protection. India's Ayurvedic knowledge protected not only India but the entire world, showcasing the power of Ayurveda globally.

The global pharmaceutical trade is worth ₹500 trillion.

Since we abandoned Ayurveda for modern medicine, India has become the world's most ill country. If we focus on Ayurveda, it presents a tremendous opportunity for India. Currently, India spends 2.6% of its GDP on medical and health expenses, whereas other countries spend 8-9%.

India exports only 2.6% of the world's medicines, amounting to approximately $22 billion. However, India imports 80% of its raw pharmaceutical ingredients from China, which is a significant issue that needs to be addressed promptly. To avoid this problem, it is crucial to consume organic food, as many doctors say our body becomes what we eat.

The question here is what the relationship between agriculture and medicines is. Now, let's discuss the Ayurvedic herbs and crops used in traditional Indian medicine in detail.

The global trade of herbs is worth $216 billion, and it is estimated to grow to $440 billion by 2032. According to the WHO, the trade in herbs is growing at 15% annually. After COVID-19, the popularity of herbs has increased significantly worldwide, leading to substantial growth in their trade. The demand for herbs is very high, but their production is limited. After China, India is the world's second-largest exporter of herbs. Together, China and India fulfill 70% of the global demand for herbs. India's biodiversity is such that it produces the highest quality herbs globally. The world has 16 climatic zones, and India is the only country where all 16 climates are found, such as rainforests in Meghalaya, deserts in Rajasthan, and Himalayan regions in North India. Due to these diverse climates, India produces a wide variety of fruits, vegetables, spices, pulses, and herbs of excellent quality and quantity.

In the Himalayas alone, the Gandhamardan mountain range contains over 16,000 rare herbs.

The Future of Bamboo Trade

The global bamboo trade is worth $65 billion annually and is expected to reach $94 billion by 2030.

Investment and Return on Investment (ROI) in Bamboo:

- Investment Example: If you invest ₹1.5 million in 10 acres of bamboo plantation, after 5 years, you can earn ₹1.5 million annually for up to 70 years.
- ROI: This means a return of ₹105 million on an investment of ₹1.5 million.

Notable Bamboo Projects:

- The first 80-story bamboo tower in London.
- The world's tallest bamboo tower is under construction in Tokyo.

Products Made from Bamboo:

- Wood Industry
- Forestry
- Pulp and Paper Industry
- Textile Industry
- Bioenergy Industry
- Food and Beverage Industry
- Automotive Industry
- And much more

India imports bamboo worth ₹2,400 crores annually. China is the largest exporter of bamboo.

Thus, by investing in bamboo, industrialists and farmers can earn significant profits, thereby strengthening the Indian economy.

Future of the Sandalwood Business

The sandalwood business is valued at $300 million annually.

International Demand:

- The international demand for sandalwood is estimated to be approximately 10,000 metric tons per year.
- High demand and low supply:
- The annual global demand for Indian sandalwood is 28,000 tons.
- The legal annual supply of Indian sandalwood is only 200 tons.
- There has been a 90% decline in the official supply of sandalwood in the last 10 years.
- The natural population of sandalwood is nearly depleted.

Popularity:

- Indian sandalwood is the most popular worldwide.
- Australia is the largest producer of Indian sandalwood.
- The Australian company Galderma sells sandalwood oil at $5000 per kilogram.

Products Made from Sandalwood:

- Superior furniture and handicrafts
- Indian sandalwood core logs
- Religious rituals and ceremonies
- Medicines
- Perfumes
- Cosmetics
- Natural medicine
- Aromatherapy

Sandalwood Cultivation:

Investment and Returns:
- Investment: ₹1.5 million
- Returns: ₹25 million in 10 years
  Planting and Costs for 1 Acre:
- High demand and low supply
- White sandalwood: 375 plants
- Kaurina: 125 plants
- Native neem: 125 plants
- Red sandalwood: 125 plants
- Sweet neem: 750 plants
- Drip irrigation
- Solar electric fencing
- Annual weeding and soil tilling
- Organic fertilizers
- Security and labor costs
  Estimated Investment:
- The estimated investment over 10 years will be ₹1.2 to ₹1.8 million depending on location, soil health, etc.
- If land is required, we can assist as per your needs or arrange for rental.

Industrial Hemp

The global cannabis market size was $5.7 billion in 2021 and is expected to grow from $6.54 billion in 2022 to $18.71 billion by 2030 at a CAGR of 14.04% during the forecast period (2023-2030).

Medical cannabis is permitted under national law through licenses, and CBD oil manufactured under the Drugs and Cosmetics Act can be legally obtained and used. According to the Drugs and Cosmetics Act, legal cannabis should not contain more than 0.3 percent THC.

High Demand and Low Supply:

- Cannabis is also known as marijuana and CBD.
- Canada is the largest exporter of cannabis oil.
- In 2022, Canada exported 514 metric tons of hemp oil to several trade partners, including New Zealand and South Korea, with a total value

exceeding $4.5 million. The total export volume of hemp oil to the United States was 403 metric tons, valued at $3.8 million.

- China has made significant investments and research in cannabis over the past five years.
- Globally, there are 606 patents related to cannabis, of which China holds 309.
- This year, Thailand and Malaysia legalized cannabis.
- Worldwide, 34 countries have allowed cannabis for medicinal and therapeutic use.
- China has become a powerhouse in cannabis plant production.
- Germany became the world's largest medical cannabis market this year.
- The USA and other major countries have legalized it and made significant investments.

Economic Potential:

- Cannabis can bring in an income of more than ₹105,000 ($1,500) per hectare.
- Levi's first jeans and jacket were made from 69% cotton and 31% hemp.

Status in India:

- Some parts of cannabis are legal in India.
- With more information gathering, research and development, and an investment of ₹1 trillion, this can become a significant business for India in the next few years.
- The Indian Himalayas, particularly Uttarakhand, provide the best land for cannabis cultivation.

Global Textile Trade

Market Valuation:

- In 2023, the global textile market was valued at $1,837.27 billion.
- It is expected to grow at a compound annual growth rate (CAGR) of 7.4% from 2024 to 2030.

Historical Context:

- Before the 1800s, India had a monopoly in the textile sector.
- India's textile and apparel industry contributes approximately 2.3% to the country's GDP, 13% to industrial production, and 12% to exports.
- The textile industry employs around 45 million people directly and indirectly, making it the second-largest provider of employment in India after agriculture.

Key Facts:

- Jute: India is the largest producer of jute, accounting for about 62.2% of the world's production and 59.3% of the total area. In the fiscal year 2022, India produced over one million metric tons of jute from around 660 thousand hectares. India is also the second-largest exporter of jute products in the world.
- Silk: India is the second-largest producer of silk in the world.
- Cotton: India is the largest producer of cotton globally. In 2022-2023, India produced 5.84 million metric tons of cotton, which is 23.83% of the world's total cotton production. India is also the second-largest producer of fiber in the world.

Economic Comparison:

- The French company Christian Dior has a turnover of €86.2 billion, which is more than India's total textile exports.
- India's textile exports amount to only $45 billion.

Emerging Trends:

- Many companies worldwide are beginning to produce hemp, bamboo, and organic cotton textiles.
- The fashion industry is the second most polluting industry after oil.

Monsanto's Bt Cotton Seeds:

- 90% of India's cotton and 80% of China's cotton use Bt cotton.
- India is the second-largest producer of cotton globally, after China.
- Over 300,000 farmers in India have committed suicide following the massive failure of Monsanto's Bt cotton seeds.
- Globally, around one million people commit suicide each year.

Issues and Solutions:

- Through seed patents, Monsanto has become the "life god" of our planet, charging farmers and original breeders for the renewal of life.
- By starting organic textile farming, using organic seeds, hemp textiles, and bamboo textiles, India can save its farmers, safeguard the country, and contribute to global sustainability.

Global Construction Business

Market Valuation:

- The current and approved value of the global construction business is $15.97 trillion.

Technology: Cement vs. Limestone (Lime):

- Cement: Maximum lifespan of 100 years.
- Limestone: Minimum lifespan of 500 years.

Production Capacity:

- By 2024, the cement production capacity is expected to be 1 billion tons per year.
- India is the world's second-largest producer of cement.

Environmental Impact:

- Ordinary cement typically produces 89-90 calories/gram in 7 days and 90-100 calories/gram in 28 days.
- Cement construction materials account for 9% of global carbon dioxide emissions, which is more than all the carbon dioxide produced by trucks worldwide.

Durability Concerns:

- Structures like the Vashi Bridge near Mumbai and the Mandovi River Bridge in Goa, as well as overhead tanks and multistory concrete residential buildings, have shown sustainability issues.
- Indian limestone technology is among the oldest in the world.

Benefits of Limestone Technology:

- Temples in India constructed using limestone technology are over 5000 years old. The Ram Setu Bridge is approximately 10,000 years old.
- Buildings coated with lime can experience up to 9% cooler temperatures inside.

Economic Implications:

- Continuous use of cement will result in spending the entire nation's money on reconstruction every 100 years.

Recommendations:

- Start using limestone, bamboo, hempcrete, and self-healing concrete to save India and the world.
- The British eradicated limestone technology in India.
- The British discouraged the use of indigenous materials or systems like Dhaka muslin, handloom weaving, Ayurveda, and the Gurukul system, and offered their imported versions instead, aiming to eliminate old Indian indigenous systems.
- The use of lime in construction also faced a similar fate during their rule.

By adopting sustainable building materials and technologies, India can ensure long-lasting infrastructure and reduce environmental impact.

Global Logistics Market Size

The global logistics market size was valued at $7.98 trillion in 2022 and is expected to reach approximately $18.23 trillion by 2030, growing at a remarkable CAGR of 10.7% from 2023 to 2030.

Key Insights:

- According to MarketLine, road freight and logistics represent the leading segment in the global transport services market, accounting for over 74% of the total industry value.
- The global freight sector is projected to reach over 12.4 trillion FTKs (freight tonne-kilometers) in volume.
- In terms of value, the road freight sector in the United States accounts for 56% of the world's road freight market.

Impact on Global Warming:

- The freight sector significantly contributes to global warming due to its extensive use of fossil fuels and resulting carbon emissions.

Recommendations:

- Think Global, Stay Local - Buy Local:
- Supporting local businesses and buying locally available products can boost the local economy.
- Avoiding online purchases for locally available products helps reduce transportation emissions and supports local employment.
- A strong local economy is essential for the sustainable development of India.

From Plastic to Petrol/Biodiesel

Key Facts:

- Between 1950 and 2019, 830 million tons of plastic waste was generated.
- Only 10% of plastic is recycled, while 90% is discarded.
- Millions of tons of plastic are used daily.

Opportunity:

- Converting end-grade plastic to petrol/biodiesel and other fuels.
- Project cost ranges from ₹1 million to ₹100 million to start the business.

Polyhydroxybutyrate (PHB)

Description:
- PHB is a biodegradable polymer produced by bacteria and archaea as an energy and carbon reserve.

- It belongs to the microbial polyester family of polyhydroxyalkanoates (PHAs). PHB is synthesized in microbial cells, such as Gram-positive and Gram-negative bacteria, when they experience nutrient stress or adverse environments.

Characteristics:

- PHB is a rigid and brittle polymer with thermoplastic, hydrophobic, and highly crystalline properties.
- It is produced through a sequence of three enzymatic reactions catalyzed by β-ketothiolase, acetoacetyl-CoA reductase, and PHB synthase from acetyl-CoA.

Production:

- PHB is primarily a product of carbon assimilation from glucose or starch, and microorganisms use it as an energy storage molecule when other common energy sources are not available.
  Applications:
- PHB has properties similar to various synthetic thermoplastics like polypropylene, making it useful for a wide range of applications and the future commercial large-scale production of biodegradable plastics.

Why Are We Talking About Agriculture in the Age of AI?

You might be wondering why we are discussing agriculture in the age of AI. When it comes to India, our ancestors made decisions after carefully assessing long-term benefits and risks. India's excellent education system taught us not to sacrifice long-term gains for short-term profits. While we might have endured some losses, we always planned for a bright future for our upcoming generations.

Today, people consider agriculture a simple profession and are investing billions in AI. However, in the race to make quick money, we cannot fulfill the fundamental needs of humanity.

Lessons from the Green Revolution:

In our haste to advance agriculture, we indiscriminately used chemicals and fertilizers post the Green Revolution of the 1960s. Over the past 65 years, we have destroyed 70% of arable land, and 7 out of 10 people have become ill. Today, the world is selling expensive agricultural products under the label of organic farming, which we used to produce at a much lower cost through traditional agriculture.

A scientific report has revealed that due to mobile radiation, in the next 50 years, 9 out of 10 children will be physically and mentally handicapped. Just as the use of chemicals has crippled agriculture, we now have an opportunity to lay the foundation for a sustainable future.

Disadvantages of Artificial Intelligence

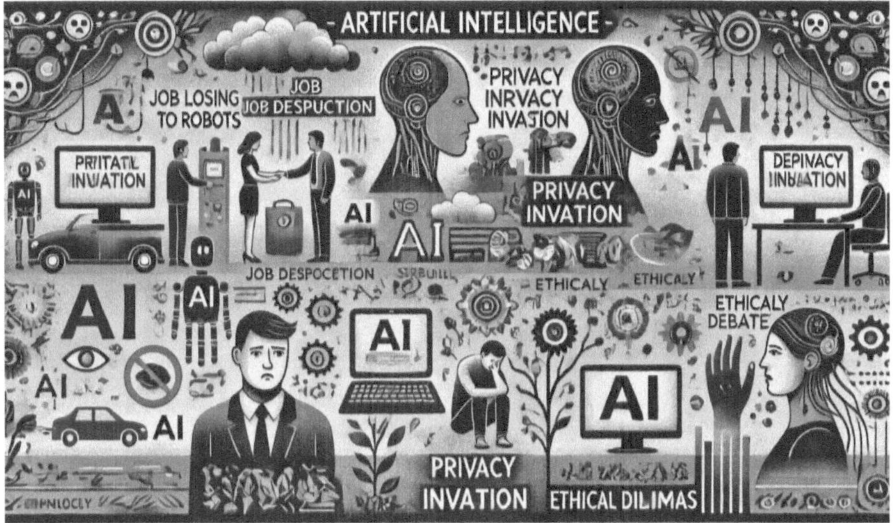

1. High Costs:

- Building machines that can simulate human intelligence is a significant achievement that requires a lot of time, resources, and money. AI needs the latest hardware and software to stay updated and meet current requirements, making it quite expensive.

2. Lack of Creativity:

- AI cannot think outside the box. It can learn over time with pre-fed data and past experiences but cannot be creative in its approach. For example, bots like Quill can write earnings reports for Forbes based only on pre-existing data and facts. While impressive, these reports lack the human touch present in other Forbes articles.

3. Unemployment:

- One application of AI is robots, which are displacing jobs and increasing unemployment in some cases. For instance, in technologically advanced countries like Japan, robots often replace human resources in manufacturing businesses. However, this is not always the case, as it also creates additional opportunities for humans to work while replacing them to increase efficiency.

4. Makes Humans Lazy:

- AI applications automate most tedious and repetitive tasks, reducing our need to use our minds. This addiction to AI can create problems for future generations.

5. No Ethics:

- Ethics and morality are important human traits that can be challenging to incorporate into AI. Rapid AI advancement has raised concerns that one day, AI might grow uncontrollably and eventually wipe out humanity, known as AI singularity.

6. Emotionless:

- From childhood, we are taught that neither computers nor other machines have emotions. Humans work as a team, and team management is essential for achieving goals. Although robots are more efficient than humans, the human connections that form the basis of teams cannot be replaced by computers.

7. No Improvement:

- Humans cannot develop AI beyond the pre-loaded facts and experience-based technology. AI is efficient in performing repetitive tasks, but if we want any adjustment or improvement, we must manually change the code. AI cannot access and use human intelligence, but it can store infinite data. Machines can only complete the tasks they are developed or programmed for; if asked to do something else, they often fail or produce useless results, which can have significant negative impacts.

AI in Healthcare

AI in healthcare presents ethical and privacy concerns. AI systems in healthcare rely heavily on patient data, including sensitive medical information. Ensuring this data is collected, stored, and used securely and with privacy in mind is crucial. Protecting patient privacy, maintaining data confidentiality, and preventing unauthorized access to personal health information are essential considerations.

AI in Marketing

A downside of AI in marketing is the potential lack of a human touch and creativity. While AI can automate various marketing tasks and generate data-driven insights, it struggles to replicate the unique human elements of marketing, such as emotional connections, intuition, and creative thinking. AI algorithms may rely heavily on data and predefined patterns, potentially missing out on innovative or out-of-the-box marketing approaches that require human creativity and intuition.

AI in Education

AI in education raises potential ethical and privacy concerns. AI systems collect and analyze significant amounts of data on students' performance, behavior, and personal information. Ensuring this data is handled securely with appropriate privacy protection measures is necessary.

AI in Creativity

A drawback of AI in creativity is the potential lack of originality and authenticity in AI-generated creative works. While AI systems can mimic existing styles and patterns, there is debate about whether AI can genuinely possess creativity similar to humans. AI-generated works may lack the depth, emotional engagement, and unique perspectives from human experiences and emotions.

AI in Transportation

The disadvantage of AI in transportation lies in the ethical and legal challenges it presents. For instance, autonomous vehicles raise questions about liability in accidents. Determining responsibility when an AI-controlled vehicle is involved in a collision can be complex. Additionally, AI systems' decisions related to traffic management or accident avoidance may require considering ethical factors, such as allocating limited resources or balancing passengers' safety versus pedestrians. Balancing these ethical dilemmas and developing appropriate regulations and guidelines for AI in transportation is a complex and ongoing challenge.

Conclusion

While AI offers significant advantages and transformative potential across various sectors, it is essential to recognize and address its limitations and challenges. A balanced approach that considers both AI's benefits and drawbacks can help us build a sustainable future while preserving humanity's fundamental needs and values.

Soil

The value of soil is many times greater than that of gold and diamonds. If we do not protect and preserve our soil, we will destroy not only the soil but also ourselves. If there were no shortage of food, water, and employment in the world, there would be no wars, no terrorism, and no poverty.

If we fail to save our soil, the entire world will be destroyed.

Current Situation:

According to the United Nations Food and Agriculture Organization, the world has only 60 years of farming left, and to meet the global food supply, farmers need 6 million hectares of new fertile land each year.

Problem:

Each year, 12 million hectares of land become unsuitable for farming due to the use of chemical fertilizers and pesticides.

Situation in India:

The biggest tragedy in India is that despite being a predominantly Hindu nation, cows are being slaughtered. If cows are protected, their dung can be used to produce indigenous fertilizer, which can turn barren land fertile without any chemical fertilizers. This can significantly increase crop yields and help alleviate the global food crisis.

Global Perspective:

The world is currently searching for life on the moon and other planets, but no effort is being made to save the Earth we have.

Solution:

If cows are protected, the country and the world will be protected. Organic food and seeds will become available, which will not only eliminate poverty in the country but also reduce diseases by up to 80%.

Will Organic Farming Disappear in India?

The question arises: Will organic farming disappear in India, or is there an alternative?

There is a possibility of developing a type of farming in India that could attract industrialists. Large industrialists are fully capable; they have lands and can make substantial investments in agriculture. They can afford to wait 5 to 10 years for special crops. Indian farmers, however, are not in a position to wait 5 years for profits. Can we create an agricultural business model where industrialists and farmers together can lay the foundation for a new India?

Since we have abandoned the principles of 5G (Gayatri Mantra, Gita, Guru, Ganga, and Gaumata), our country has lost its unique identity in the world.

Challenges in Current Agriculture:

In India's ancient traditional agricultural system, cow dung manure was considered the best fertilizer. However, the problem today is that despite being a predominantly Hindu nation, countless innocent cows are being slaughtered for the meat trade.

- Bulls Protection: As long as bullock carts were in use, bulls were protected. With modernization, the use of bullock carts has decreased, leading to the slaughter of many bulls.
- Cow Utilization: Cows are only used until they give milk; once they stop giving milk, they are often left to be slaughtered because the number of farmers has decreased significantly.
- Chemical Fertilizers: Farmers can no longer keep cows as they used to because chemical fertilizers have replaced cow dung manure.

Proposed Solution:

If we return to traditional agricultural systems, it is possible to protect cows. The current shortage of cows will not be sufficient to meet the demand for cow dung manure. Therefore, we need to build a public cowshed in each village.

- Public Cowsheds: Bulls, cows, buffaloes, and other animals that farmers can no longer use can be gathered in these cowsheds, and their dung can be used to make manure. This manure can be used for farming, providing the village with a supply of organic fertilizer.
- Animal Protection: This initiative will help protect animals like cows and bulls.
- Traditional Organic Farming: Returning to traditional organic farming will lead to higher production and help prevent diseases.

Attracting Industrialists:

We can develop an agricultural business model that involves both industrialists and farmers.

- Investment and Partnership: Industrialists can invest in large-scale organic farming projects and work in partnership with farmers.
- Long-term Vision: This model will involve long-term planning and investment, with the understanding that organic farming may take several years to become profitable.

- Mutual Benefit: Such a model would benefit both parties: industrialists can achieve substantial returns on their investments, and farmers can gain access to resources and support they would not have on their own.

By creating a collaborative approach between industrialists and farmers, we can ensure the sustainability of organic farming in India and lay the foundation for a healthier, more prosperous future.

Key Requirements for Farming

Farming primarily requires four main things: land, seeds, water, and fertilizer. A detailed explanation regarding land and fertilizer has already been provided. Now, we aim to create the world's largest seed bank across India, so that every farmer can access seeds for free. Additionally, in collaboration with organizations like the Water Foundation, we plan to ensure water supply in every village. These efforts can help make India a robust nation with a rich heritage in organic agriculture.

Mantras for Success

Many students and others often ask me the secret of my success. I attribute my entire success to my Lord Shri RadhaMadhav and my parents. Nowadays, many people, after receiving a little education, deny the existence of God and abandon their parents in old age homes. This is extremely unfortunate for a culturally rich country like India.

We should always respect and serve our parents, teachers, elders, and God. It is through their blessings that we can achieve success in life. Parents and teachers are our first guides in life. Their experiences and teachings inspire us to move forward in the right direction.

Faith in God provides us with strength and mental peace. Believing in God gives us the power to face life's challenges. Serving and receiving blessings from our elders provides us with positive energy, which motivates us to progress in life.

I believe that by adhering to the principles of service, respect, and faith, we can achieve not only personal success but also build a prosperous and harmonious society. Therefore, we should all respect and serve our parents, teachers, and God, so that their blessings continue to guide our lives.

Source

- Https://www.stephen-knapp.com/
- https://www.researchgate.net/
- https://en.wikipedia.org/wiki/List_of_Indian_inventions_and_discoveries
- https://books.google.com/
- And many spiritual books

भारत

अतीत का नायक - भविष्य का नेता

डॉ. लाल तनवानी

विषयसूची

परिचय

डॉ. लाल एन. तानवानी: शिक्षा और शिक्षण को समर्पित एक जीवन

मेरा नाम डॉ. लाल एन. तानवानी है, लेकिन कई लोग मुझे लाल सर के नाम से जानते हैं। मैंने अपने जीवन को ज्ञान और शैक्षणिक उत्कृष्टता के प्रति समर्पित कर दिया है। वर्षों से, मुझे सबसे अधिक शैक्षिक डिग्रियाँ प्राप्त करने के लिए विश्व रिकॉर्ड में मान्यता मिली है, जैसा कि वर्ल्ड बुक ऑफ रिकॉर्ड्स लंदन, एशिया बुक ऑफ रिकॉर्ड्स, इंटरनेशनल बुक ऑफ वर्ल्ड रिकॉर्ड्स ब्रावो, और इंडिया बुक ऑफ रिकॉर्ड्स द्वारा दर्ज किया गया है।

मेरी शैक्षिक यात्रा 1991 में शुरू हुई और यह एक विविध और समृद्ध अनुभव रहा है। मेरी योग्यताएँ निम्नलिखित हैं:

- बी.कॉम.
- एम.कॉम. (वित्त)
- बी.एड.
- एम.कॉम. (लागत लेखा)
- एम.ए. (अर्थशास्त्र)
- एम.फिल. (वाणिज्य)
- पी.एच.डी. (वाणिज्य)
- एमबीए (वित्त)
- वैल्यू एजुकेशन में एडवांस डिप्लोमा
- डी.लिट.
- पी.एच.डी. (प्रबंधन)

ये डिग्रियाँ निरंतर सीखने के प्रति मेरी प्रतिबद्धता और विभिन्न विषयों में व्यापक समझ प्राप्त करने की मेरी इच्छा को दर्शाती हैं।

मेरी व्यक्तिगत शैक्षिक उपलब्धियों के अलावा, मैं शिक्षा और उद्यमिता में गहराई से शामिल हूँ। पद्मा कोचिंग क्लासेस के सीईओ और पद्मा इंस्टीट्यूट ऑफ नॉलेज एंड रिसर्च के प्रोग्राम निदेशक के रूप में, मैं छात्रों को उनके शैक्षणिक प्रयासों में सशक्त बनाने का प्रयास करता हूँ। मैं एनसीटी कॉन्वेंट स्कूल और बीबीआरटी इंटरनेशनल स्कूल के संस्थापक ट्रस्टी, और नव जीवन को-ऑप बैंक लिमिटेड के निदेशक के रूप में भी कार्यरत हूँ। मेरे संस्थान वाणिज्य, बैंकिंग, वित्त और प्रबंधन के क्षेत्रों में प्रतिभाओं को पोषित करने पर ध्यान केंद्रित करते हैं।

2024 में, मैंने पद्मा इंटरनेशनल प्रीस्कूल की स्थापना की, जहाँ हम ब्रिटिश पाठ्यक्रम को भारतीय मूल्यों और विरासत के साथ मिलाते हैं। यहाँ, हम तीन साल की उम्र से ही छात्रों को आवश्यक कौशल का प्रशिक्षण देते हैं।

कक्षा के बाहर भी शिक्षा के प्रति मेरा जुनून है। मैंने राष्ट्रीय और अंतर्राष्ट्रीय स्तर पर कई सम्मेलनों और कार्यशालाओं में सक्रिय रूप से भाग लिया है, और मैं निरंतर सीखने का प्रबल समर्थक हूँ। 30 से अधिक वर्षों के शिक्षण अनुभव के साथ, मैंने तेज़-तर्रार वातावरण में छात्रों की आवश्यकताओं को पूरा करने के लिए अपनी कौशल को निखारा है, हमेशा उच्चतम स्तर की अखंडता और गोपनीयता बनाए रखी है।

मेरी कहानी समर्पण, दृढ़ता, और ज्ञान की असीम खोज की है। मैं छात्रों और शिक्षकों दोनों को प्रेरित करना चाहता हूँ, यह प्रदर्शित करते हुए कि सीखना एक जीवनभर की यात्रा है जो किसी भी सीमा को नहीं जानती।

पुरस्कार और उपलब्धियाँ

अपने करियर के दौरान, मुझे भारत और अंतरराष्ट्रीय स्तर पर कई पुरस्कारों से सम्मानित किया गया है। मेरे कुछ उल्लेखनीय पुरस्कार निम्नलिखित हैं:

- इंटरनेशनल बुक ऑफ वर्ल्ड रिकॉर्ड्स ब्रावो 2023
- "व्यक्तिगत द्वारा प्राप्त की गई अधिकतम शैक्षिक डिग्रियाँ" भारत बुक ऑफ रिकॉर्ड्स 2021
- "ग्रैंडमास्टर सर्टिफिकेशन" एशिया बुक ऑफ रिकॉर्ड्स 2021
- "व्यक्तिगत द्वारा धारित अधिकतम शैक्षिक डिग्रियाँ" वर्ल्ड बुक ऑफ रिकॉर्ड्स, लंदन 2021
- "नेल्सन मंडेला नोबेल पीस अवार्ड 2020" शिक्षा और सामाजिक कार्यकर्ता के लिए
- "सर्टिफिकेट ऑफ एक्सीलेंस 2020" "भारत को स्थायी विकसित और मजबूत बनाने के लिए वैश्विक शांति" के लिए द अमेरिकन यूनिवर्सिटी द्वारा
- 2019 इंडो एशिया अवार्ड फॉर एक्सीलेंस इन एजुकेशन, दुबई (यू.ए.ई.)
- "इंटरनेशनल एचीवर्स अवार्ड 2018 फॉर एजुकेशन एक्सीलेंस", थाईलैंड
- "आउटस्टैंडिंग रिसर्च पेपर अवार्ड" मुंबई विश्वविद्यालय द्वारा 2018
- डॉ. ए. पी. जे. अब्दुल कलाम लाइफटाइम अचीवमेंट अवार्ड 2018 अंतर्राष्ट्रीय सामाजिक और आर्थिक सुधार संस्थान, बेंगलुरु द्वारा
- ईटी बिजनेस आइकन्स नील नितिन मुकेश द्वारा 2020 में
- 2018 में मुंबई विश्वविद्यालय द्वारा सर्वश्रेष्ठ शिक्षक के लिए प्रशस्ति पत्र
- भारत रत्न डॉ. राधाकृष्णन गोल्ड मेडल अवार्ड 2018, चेन्नई
- शिक्षा भारती पुरस्कार 2017, नई दिल्ली
- "सर्वश्रेष्ठ शिक्षण पुरस्कार 2017" भारतीय शिक्षा पुरस्कार, दिल्ली द्वारा

आयोजित पद

- वर्षों में, मैंने कई महत्वपूर्ण पदों पर कार्य किया है:
- बीबीआरटी इंटरनेशनल स्कूल के संस्थापक ट्रस्टी
- एनसीटी कॉन्वेंट स्कूल, उल्हासनगर के संस्थापक ट्रस्टी
- जयवंती नोटंदास तानवानी चैरिटेबल ट्रस्ट के संस्थापक
- पद्मा कोचिंग क्लासेस के सीईओ
- पद्मा इंस्टीट्यूट ऑफ नॉलेज एंड रिसर्च के कार्यक्रम निदेशक
- नव जीवन को-ऑप बैंक लिमिटेड में निदेशक
- झूलेलाल ट्रस्ट स्कूल, उल्हासनगर के पूर्व शैक्षिक निदेशक

- रोटरी क्लब ऑफ उल्हासनगर मिडटाउन के पूर्व अध्यक्ष
- लायंस क्लब, उल्हासनगर के पूर्व अध्यक्ष
- ओरिएंटल इंस्टीट्यूट ऑफ मैनेजमेंट, वाशी में व्याख्याता
- बिरला कॉलेज, कल्याण में व्याख्याता

मेरी यात्रा शिक्षा की परिवर्तनकारी शक्ति का प्रमाण है। मुझे उम्मीद है कि मैं दूसरों को उसी जुनून और समर्पण के साथ ज्ञान और व्यक्तिगत विकास की तलाश करने के लिए प्रेरित कर सकता हूँ।

वैदिक संस्कृति का परिचय

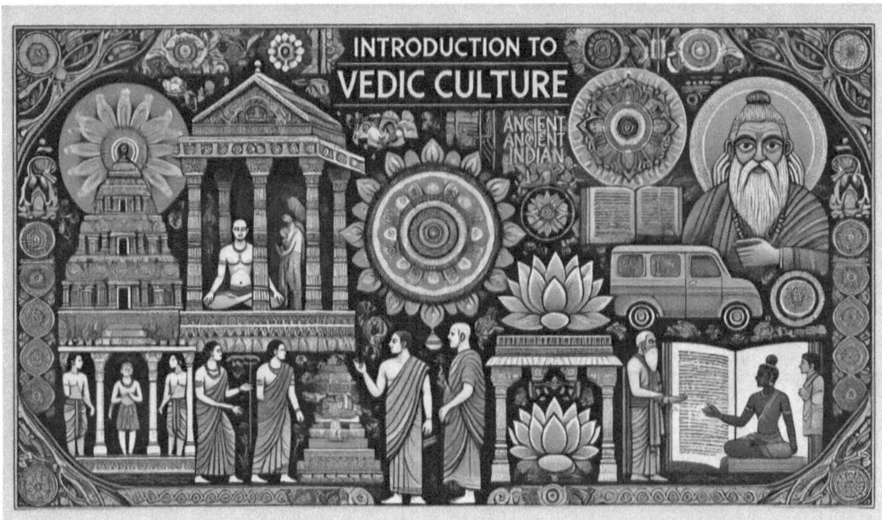

भारत के बारे में एक अज्ञात तथ्य यह है कि प्रारंभिक सभ्यता का योगदान शायद ही अब तक अकादमिक शिक्षा का हिस्सा रहा है। आइए हम भारत की उत्कृष्ट वैदिक संस्कृति और संपूर्ण विश्व में इसके सर्वोच्च योगदान के बारे में समझें जो आज भी अपने तरीके से विद्यमान है। हिंदू संस्कृति अपनी आध्यात्मिकता के लिए प्रसिद्ध है। हालाँकि, विज्ञान, प्रौद्योगिकी और उद्योग भी इस संस्कृति से बहुत जुड़े हुए हैं।

लोगों को हिंदू संस्कृति के अन्य तथ्यों के बारे में नहीं पता होने का कारण यह है कि, श्री धर्मपाल और अन्य प्रसिद्ध लेखकों के हालिया शोध के अनुसार, औपनिवेशिक शासक हिंदू संस्कृति के सभी सकारात्मक पहलुओं के बारे में जानकारी को नष्ट करना चाहते थे। 18वीं शताब्दी के अंत तक भारत विश्व की औद्योगिक कार्यशाला था। हिंदुओं ने खगोल विज्ञान के सिद्धांतों की मूल बातें, मौलिक कण, ब्रह्मांड की उत्पत्ति, व्यावहारिक मनोचिकित्सा इत्यादि के साथ शुरुआत की थी, जो अच्छी तरह से दर्ज नहीं हैं और लोकप्रिय रूप से ज्ञात नहीं हैं।

प्राचीन हिंदुओं के पास कपड़ा इंजीनियरिंग, चीनी मिट्टी की चीज़ें, मुद्रण, हथियार, जलवायु विज्ञान और मौसम विज्ञान, वास्तुकला, चिकित्सा और सर्जरी, धातु विज्ञान, कृषि और कृषि इंजीनियरिंग, सिविल इंजीनियरिंग, नगर नियोजन और इसी तरह के अन्य क्षेत्रों में अत्यधिक विकसित प्रौद्योगिकियां थीं, जिसके बारे में अब शायद ही किसी को पता हो। एक और तथ्य यह है कि, हिंदुओं को इस बारे में बहुत ज्ञान था कि सूर्य सौरमंडल का केंद्र है, पृथ्वी के भूगोल के बारे में, पौधे किस प्रकार भोजन उत्पन्न करते हैं, शरीर में रक्त का संचार कैसे होता है, विज्ञान, गणित और संख्याओं के बारे में, स्वास्थ्य, चिकित्सा और शल्य चिकित्सा आदि के सिद्धांत।

बहुमूल्य संस्कृति और महान भारतीय सभ्यता को विदेशों के महान लेखकों और साहित्यकारों ने भी मान्यता दी है। अरब विद्वान सईद इब्न अहमद अल-अंदालुसी (1029-1070) ने विज्ञान पर अपने इतिहास में, जिसे तबकात-अल-उमाम कहा जाता है, लिखा है:

"भारत में विज्ञान लॉन्च करने वाला पहला राष्ट्र... भारत अपने लोगों की बुद्धिमत्ता के लिए जाना जाता है। कई शताब्दियों में, अतीत के सभी राजाओं ने ज्ञान की सभी शाखाओं में भारतीयों की क्षमता को पहचाना है।"

अमेरिकी प्रोफेसर जाबेज़ टी. सुंदरलैंड (1842-1936), अमेरिका के भारत सूचना ब्यूरो के अध्यक्ष ने भारत में कई वर्ष बिताए। वह इंडिया इन बॉन्डेज के लेखक थे, जिसमें उन्होंने लिखा था,

"भारत ने सभी विज्ञानों की शुरुआत की और उनमें से कुछ को विकास की उल्लेखनीय डिग्री तक पहुंचाया, जिससे दुनिया का नेतृत्व हुआ। भारत ने महान साहित्य, महान कलाएँ, महान दार्शनिक प्रणालियाँ, महान धर्म और जीवन के हर विभाग में महान व्यक्तियों का निर्माण किया है - शासक, राजनेता, वित्तपोषक, विद्वान, कवि, उपनिवेशवादी, हर तरह के कुशल कारीगर और शिल्पकार, कृषिविद्, औद्योगिक आयोजक, और दूरगामी व्यापार और वाणिज्य में अग्रणी।"

इसके कपड़ा सामान - कपास, ऊन, लिनन और रेशम में इसके करघे के बढ़िया उत्पाद - सभ्य दुनिया में प्रसिद्ध थे; वैसे ही इसके सुंदर आभूषण और कीमती पत्थर थे, जो हर सुंदर रूप में काटे गए थे; हर प्रकार, गुणवत्ता, रंग और सुंदर आकार के मिट्टी के बर्तन, चीनी मिट्टी की चीज़ें; लोहा, इस्पात, चाँदी और सोने में बढ़िया काम। इसकी वास्तुकला बहुत अच्छी थी।

लोकप्रिय अमेरिकी लेखक मार्क ट्वेन की भी भारत के बारे में उच्च राय थी और उन्होंने लिखा,

"इसमें भौतिक संपदा का पहला संग्रह था; यह गहरे विचारकों और बुद्धिजीवियों से भरा हुआ था; इसमें खदानें, जंगल और उपजाऊ मिट्टी थी।"

डिक टेरेसी यह भी स्वीकार करते हैं कि आज हम जो ज्ञान समझते हैं, वह जरूरी नहीं कि ग्रीक सभ्यता से आया हो, बल्कि वास्तव में भारत की वैदिक परंपराओं में बहुत पहले से मौजूद था।

"बिशप हेबर ने कहा: 'जिन भी लोगों से मैं मिला हूं, उनकी तुलना में हिंदू बहादुर, बुद्धिमान, धैर्यवान और ज्ञान और सुधार के लिए सबसे अधिक उत्सुक हैं।"

गणित में योगदान

बहुत से लोगों को यह एहसास नहीं है कि प्राचीन भारत महान गणितीय विकास का जनक है। आज हम जो आनंद लेते हैं वह वैदिक सभ्यता से प्राप्त प्रारंभिक उपलब्धियों से आया है। चीनी विद्वान और लेखक लिन युतांग ने भी लिखा है कि:

"भारत त्रिकोणमिति, द्विघात समीकरण, व्याकरण, ध्वन्यात्मकता..." इत्यादि में चीन का शिक्षक था।

मिस्रवासियों के पास बड़ी गणनाओं के लिए उपयुक्त संख्यात्मक प्रणाली नहीं थी। संख्या 986 के लिए उन्हें 23 प्रतीकों का उपयोग करना पड़ा। यूनानियों के बाद, रोमन भी गणितीय गणनाओं के लिए संख्याओं की एक प्रणाली चाहते थे। दरअसल, मिस्रवासियों, बेबीलोनियों, रोमनों और यहां तक कि चीनियों की गणितीय प्रणालियाँ, सभी स्वतंत्र प्रतीकों का उपयोग कर रही थीं, जब तक कि उन्हें भारत से अंक प्रणाली की मदद नहीं मिली। उसके बाद इसे अरबी अंक कहा जाने लगा और अंततः उन्हें वह मिल गया जिसकी उन्हें आवश्यकता थी।

फ्रांस के विश्व के महानतम गणितज्ञों में से एक, पियरे लाप्लास ने लिखा:

"यह भारत ही है जिसने हमें सभी संख्याओं को दस प्रतीकों द्वारा व्यक्त करने की महान विधि दी, प्रत्येक प्रतीक को स्थिति का मान प्राप्त होता है, साथ ही एक पूर्ण मूल्य भी मिलता है। हमें इस उपलब्धि की सराहना करनी चाहिए। भारतीयों ने दुनिया भर में उपयोग किए जाने वाले संख्यात्मक आंकड़ों का आविष्कार किया। गणित में भी भारत उस समय का सबसे अधिक सभ्यता वाला देश था।"

एक उदाहरण यह है कि 2500 ईसा पूर्व के ज्यामितीय रेखांकन उपकरणों के हालिया प्रमाण सिंधु घाटी में पाए गए हैं। उस प्रारंभिक काल से प्राप्त बाट, माप और दशमलव विभाजन वाले पैमाने अभी भी काफी सटीक हैं।

यहां तक कि प्रोफेसर मोनियर विलियम्स भी अपने इंडियन विजडम (पेज 185) में कहते हैं:

"बीजगणित और ज्यामिति का आविष्कार और खगोल विज्ञान में उनका अनुप्रयोग हिंदुओं के लिए जिम्मेदार है।"

प्राचीन भारतीयों ने केवल दस चिन्हों की सहायता से किसी भी संख्या को आसानी से व्यक्त करने में सफलता प्राप्त की थी। ये अंक धीरे-धीरे उत्तरी अरब और मिस्र से होते हुए पश्चिम तक पहुंचे और 11वीं शताब्दी तक यूरोप तक पहुंच गए। यूरोपीय लोग इन्हें अरबी अंक कहते थे। लेकिन अरब स्वयं इन्हें हिंदू अंक (अल-अरकान, अलहिंदू) कहते थे।

वैदिक प्रणाली ने शून्य का भी आविष्कार किया था, जिसे गणित के इतिहास में सबसे महान विकासों में से एक कहा गया है। गणित पर सबसे पुरानी यूरोपीय पुस्तक कोडा विजिलैनस के नाम से जानी जाती है जो मैड्रिड के संग्रहालय में पाई जा सकती है। उसमें कहा गया है:

"गिनती के चिन्हों (अंकों) से हमें अनुभव होता है कि प्राचीन हिंदुओं का दिमाग बहुत तेज़ था और अन्य देश गिनती, ज्यामिति और अन्य विज्ञानों में उनसे बहुत पीछे थे। यह बात उनके नौ अंकों से सिद्ध होती है जिनकी सहायता से कोई भी संख्या लिखी जा सकती है।"

अल्बर्ट आइंस्टीन ने एक बार कहा था कि हमें भारत का आभारी होना चाहिए, जिसने हमें गिनती करना सिखाया। आर्यभट्ट ने साइन और वर्स्ड साइन (एक गणितीय शब्द) की शुरुआत की, और उन्हें बीजगणित के आविष्कारक के रूप में श्रेय दिया जाता है। वास्तव में, ऐसा कहा जाता है कि आर्यभट्ट ने सबसे पहले कहा था कि पृथ्वी प्रतिदिन अपनी धुरी पर घूमती है, और पृथ्वी सूर्य के चारों ओर घूमती है। हालाँकि, प्राचीन वैदिक ग्रंथों में इसका वर्णन कई वर्ष पहले ही कर दिया गया है। उन्होंने यह भी गणना की कि वर्ष की लंबाई 365.258 दिन होगी। इससे प्रारम्भिक वैदिक लोगों की बुद्धि एवं तेज का प्रमाण मिलता है।

ब्रह्मगुप्त पहले व्यक्ति थे जिन्होंने अपनी प्रसिद्ध पुस्तक ब्राह्मस्फुटसिद्धान्त में चक्रीय चतुर्भुज के क्षेत्रफल का सटीक सूत्र दिया था। चक्रीय चतुर्भुज के विकर्णों के लिए उनके द्वारा विकसित समीकरण भी उतने ही महत्वपूर्ण थे। ब्रह्मगुप्त ने भी न्यूटन से 500 वर्ष से भी पहले गुरुत्वाकर्षण के नियम का वर्णन किया था। उन्होंने बताया कि «प्रकृति के नियम के अनुसार सभी चीजें पृथ्वी पर गिरती हैं, चीजों को आकर्षित करना और बनाए रखना पृथ्वी की प्रकृति है।»

भास्कराचार्य ने समतल और गोलाकार त्रिकोणमिति और बीजगणित पर भी व्यापक अध्ययन किया, जिसमें समस्याओं के उल्लेखनीय समाधान थे। 17वीं और 18वीं शताब्दी तक यूरोप में इनकी खोज नहीं हुई थी। भास्कर उज्जैन खगोल विज्ञान विद्यालय से भी जुड़े हुए हैं।

माधव केरल के प्रसिद्ध गणितज्ञ और केरल गणित विद्यालय के नेता थे। पाई के लिए पावर श्रृंखला और एक अनंत श्रृंखला के रूप में साइन और कोसाइन कार्यों की खोज पर उनका काम न्यूटन से लगभग 300 साल पहले था। ये काम था 1676 में यूरोप में न्यूटन द्वारा रॉयल सोसाइटी के सचिव, हेनरी ओल्डेनबर्ग को लिखे एक पत्र में दिखाई दिया। माधव की प्रसिद्ध कृतियों में वेनवरोहा, लघु प्रकरण, स्फुट चंद्रपति (1400), अगनिता (1418), गोलावदा और महाज्ञानयान प्रकरण शामिल हैं। पहले दो कार्यों ने चंद्र गति की कठिन समस्या का समाधान दिया। बाद में, खगोलविदों ने उन्हें «क्षेत्र के स्वामी» की उपाधि दी।

सबसे पुराना इतिहास पाकिस्तान में वर्तमान कराची के उत्तर-पूर्व में स्थित मोहनजो दारो शहर के 5000 साल पुराने हिस्से में संरक्षित है। चौड़ी सड़कें, ईंटों के स्थान और टाइल वाले बाथरूम, स्विमिंग पूल वाले अपार्टमेंट घरों के प्रमाण उस समय की उन्नत सभ्यता का संकेत देते हैं। "इन शुरुआती लोगों के पास लिखने, गिनने, वजन करने और मापने की प्रणालियाँ थीं और उन्होंने सिंचाई के लिए नहरें खोदीं। इन सबके लिए बुनियादी गणित और इंजीनियरिंग की आवश्यकता थी।

यूनानी प्रभाव और उत्पत्ति को हमेशा मान्यता दी जाती है, लेकिन हिंदू योगदान को बहुत कम ही स्वीकार या उल्लेख किया जाता है। हालाँकि, भारत अभी भी अपनी बौद्धिकता के लिए जाना जाता है।

संस्कृत भाषा

निस्संदेह, वैदिक संस्कृति का सबसे बड़ा योगदान संस्कृत की लिपि और भाषा है। संस्कृत प्राचीन भारत और वैदिक दर्शन की भाषा है। यह एक आदर्श भाषा है, जिसमें जिस आध्यात्मिक स्पंदन को वह बोलता है, वह भी मौजूद है।

"संस्कृत भाषा अपनी वर्णमाला में 50 ध्वनियों और अक्षरों से बनी है। इसकी 11,000 जड़ें हैं जिनसे हम शब्द बना सकते हैं। अंग्रेजी भाषा में 500,000 शब्द हैं।

संस्कृत भाषा में 1700 धातु (मूल क्रिया), 80 उपसर्ग (प्रत्यय, उपसर्ग) और 20 प्रत्यय (विक्षेप) हैं। ऐसा माना जाता है कि संस्कृत में लगभग 74,000,000 शब्द हैं। वास्तव में, इन नियमों का उपयोग करके और उपसर्गों और प्रत्ययों को जोड़कर, संस्कृत अनंत संख्या में शब्द प्रदान कर सकती है जिनका अर्थ पूरी तरह से व्याकरणिक प्रक्रिया द्वारा निर्धारित होता है।

बांग्ला, गुरुमुखी, गुजराती, मराठी, उड़िया और 38 हिंदी भाषाएं संस्कृत से ही बनी हैं। दक्षिण की भाषाएँ संस्कृत से प्रभावित रही हैं। वाशू काउंटी नेवादा (यूएसए) ने 12 जनवरी 2008 को संस्कृत दिवस के रूप में घोषित किया।

ग्रीक, फ्रेंच, अंग्रेजी, अरबी, उर्दू, फ़ारसी, भारतीय, मायन, स्लाविक, रूसी, संस्कृत जैसी लगभग सभी भाषाओं में शब्द पाए जाते हैं। लेकिन केवल संस्कृत ही ऐसी भाषा है जिसके हर शब्द की अपनी पहचान है।

भारतीय पुरावशेषों के सात खंडों के संपादक, खंड IV में उल्लेख करते हैं कि पहले यूरोपीय संस्कृत विद्वान हैलहेड ने कहा, «ऐसा लगता है कि संस्कृत पृथ्वी की मूल भाषा थी»।

ऑस्ट्रेलियाई राष्ट्रीय विश्वविद्यालय, कैनबरा में एशियाई सभ्यता के पूर्व प्रोफेसर ए.एल. बाशम ने अपनी पुस्तक द वंडर दैट वाज़ इंडिया (पृष्ठ 390) में लिखा है:

"प्राचीन भारत की सबसे बड़ी उपलब्धियों में से एक इसकी उल्लेखनीय वर्णमाला है, जो स्वरों से शुरू होती है और उसके बाद आती है। व्यंजन, सभी को बहुत वैज्ञानिक तरीके से वर्गीकृत किया गया है।"

खगोल विज्ञान

कैसिनी और जीन-क्लाउड बेली (1736-93) के अनुसार, «हिंदुओं की सच्ची खगोलीय गणना के अनुसार, दुनिया का वर्तमान काल, कलियुग, ईसा के जन्म से कई साल पहले, 20 फरवरी को 3102 में शुरू हुआ था, 2 घंटे 27 मिनट पर। हिंदू राशि चक्र मनुष्य को सबसे पहले ज्ञात है, और पहला कैलेंडर भारत में 12,000 ईसा पूर्व के आसपास बनाया गया था।» यह बैली के हिस्टोइरे डी एस्टोनोमी एंसिएन और सोसाइटी ऑफ बाइबिलिकल आर्कियोलॉजी की कार्यवाही, दिसंबर 1901, भाग 1 में कहा गया था।

वैदिक खगोलीय समझ के कुछ शुरुआती संदर्भ यजुर्वेद जैसे ग्रंथों में पाए जा सकते हैं, जिसमें कहा गया है कि पृथ्वी सूर्य के आकर्षण (या गुरुत्वाकर्षण खिंचाव) के कारण अंतरिक्ष में बनी हुई है। अथर्ववेद में यह भी कहा गया है कि चंद्रमा अपनी रोशनी के लिए सूर्य पर निर्भर है।

खगोल विज्ञान पर अन्य उल्लेखनीय पुस्तकें थीं, जैसे वेदांग ज्योतिष, भृगु संहिता, और ज्योतिष शास्त्र। भारतीय खगोलशास्त्री अपनी स्थिति के बारे में काफी जानकार थे। वे पृथ्वी

के आकार और अन्य ग्रहों की कक्षाओं, और तारों के संबंध में चंद्रमा की स्थिति और चंद्रमा के चक्र को जानते थे।

आर्यभट्ट, अपने आर्यभटीय में, इसके लिए भी बहुमूल्य जानकारी देते हैं:

- चंद्रमा का एक चक्र 27.322 दिन का है, जबकि आधुनिक गणना भी 27.322 दिन की है।
- उन्होंने 1.881 वर्ष का मंगल का समय पाया, जिससे आधुनिक गणना सहमत है।
- आर्यभट्ट द्वारा 11.862 वर्ष की आधुनिक गणना के साथ बृहस्पति की आयु 11.861 वर्ष है।
- सूर्य का वर्ष 29.477 वर्ष है, आधुनिक गणना के अनुसार 29.458 वर्ष।

उन्नीसवीं सदी के फ्रांसीसी खगोलशास्त्री जीन-सिल्वन बेली भी प्राचीन हिंदुओं द्वारा बनाई गई खगोलीय तालिकाओं की पूर्णता से प्रभावित थे। उन्होंने कहा था, «...लगभग 4500 वर्ष पहले हिंदुओं द्वारा गणना की गई तारों की गति कैसिन और मेयर की तालिकाओं से एक मिनट भी भिन्न नहीं है (यूरोप में उन्नीसवीं शताब्दी में प्रयुक्त)।» सूर्य आकर्षित करने वाली शक्ति (इसके गुरुत्वाकर्षण खिंचाव से) और इसे विष्णु पुराण जैसी पुस्तकों में आगे वर्णित किया गया है, «वास्तव में, यह न तो सूर्य का उदय है और न ही सूर्यास्त है, यह हमेशा मौजूद है, और ये शब्द (उदय और अस्त) केवल इसकी उपस्थिति और गायब होने का संकेत देते हैं।»

प्लास्टिक सर्जरी

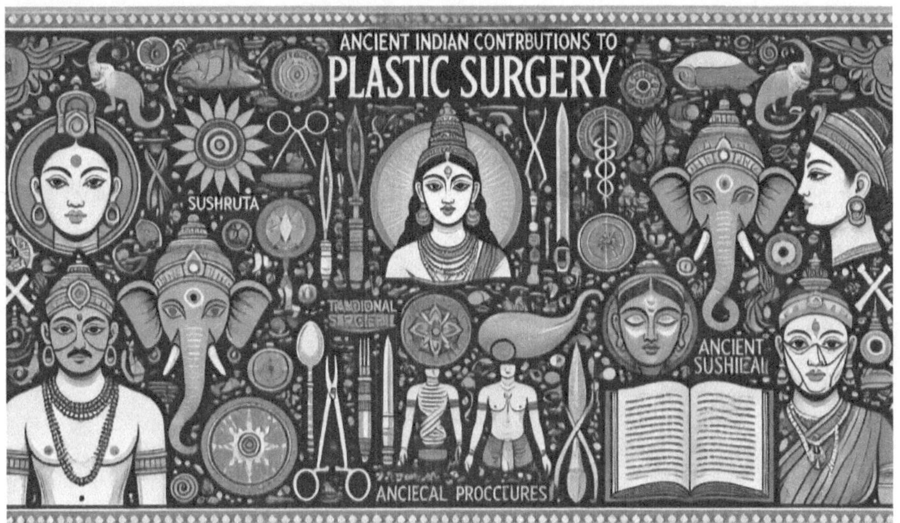

सर्जरी के संबंध में, जिसे आज हम प्लास्टिक सर्जरी के नाम से जानते हैं, वह भारत में कई वर्षों पहले से ही ज्ञात थी। इसका एक प्रमुख उदाहरण डॉ. थॉमस क्रैसो और डॉ. जेम्स फाइंडले नामक दो ब्रिटिश डॉक्टरों द्वारा देखा गया था। यह 1793 की बात है जब कावसजी नाम के एक मराठी कोचमैन को नई नाक रखनी पड़ी थी। डॉक्टरों ने इस प्रक्रिया को देखा और मद्रास गजट में चित्रों के साथ एक रिपोर्ट प्रस्तुत की, जिसे अक्टूबर 1794 संस्करण में पुनः प्रकाशित किया गया। इस रिपोर्ट ने उस समय यूरोपीय चिकित्सा जगत में प्रतिक्रियाएँ पैदा कर दीं।

नाक बदलने की पूरी प्रक्रिया, 300 से अधिक अन्य सर्जिकल ऑपरेशनों के साथ, सुश्रुत संहिता में दी गई थी। पूरे यूरोप के सर्जनों ने उपरोक्त प्रक्रिया का अध्ययन किया और विधि को समझने के बाद, 1814 में डॉ. जे.सी. कार्प्यू नामक 30 वर्षीय सर्जन ने एक आदमी की नाक का प्रत्यारोपण किया। यह ऑपरेशन भी सफल रहा। इससे शल्य चिकित्सा उपचार

में क्रांति आ गई और इसे «प्लास्टिक सर्जरी» नाम दिया गया। डॉ. कार्प्यू सहित सभी सर्जन निस्संदेह इस बात से सहमत थे कि प्लास्टिक सर्जरी प्राचीन भारत की देन है।

टीकाकरण की प्रक्रिया (मवाद को इकट्ठा करके इसे बनाना) भारत में डॉ. जेनर द्वारा किए जाने से कई साल पहले की गई थी, जिन्हें कहा जाता है कि उन्होंने 1798 में टीकाकरण की खोज की थी। पूरी प्रक्रिया को एन अकाउंट ऑफ द डिजीज ऑफ बंगाल नामक लेख में विस्तार से दिया गया था; कलकत्ता, 10 फरवरी, 1731।

जैसा कि प्राचीन भारत में विज्ञान और प्रौद्योगिकी में बी.बी. चौबे ने बताया है, «आधुनिक वैज्ञानिकों के लिए यह जानकर बहुत आश्चर्य होगा कि कई विज्ञानों के अलावा, वैदिक काल में भ्रूणविज्ञान के विकास का श्रेय भी भारत को ही जाता है।» ब्राह्मणों में यह जानने की प्रक्रिया के कई संदर्भ हैं कि नर और मादा बच्चे का जन्म कैसे होता है, अनुष्ठान संबंधी निर्देशों या निर्देशों को अर्थवाद [या अधिकार] दिया जाता है, जो वर्णन करता है कि नर या मादा को कैसे गर्भ धारण किया जाए।

वेदांग साहित्य भी इस संबंध में काफी सामग्री उपलब्ध कराता है। पुराण, विशेष रूप से गरुड़ पुराण [भागवत और अन्य के साथ] यह विवरण देता है कि एक पुरुष गर्भ में कैसे प्रकट होता है।

सुश्रुत संहिता (शरीरस्थानम, अध्यायः 5, पैराग्राफ 6) शरीर का विवरण इस प्रकार देती है:

"त्वचा की 7 परतें, 7 ऊतक, 7 पात्र, 7 तत्व, 700 नलिकाकार वाहिकाएं, 500 मांसपेशियां, 900 नसें, 300 हड्डियां, 210 जोड़, 107 महत्वपूर्ण अंग, 24 (रक्त) वाहिकाएं, 3 हास्य, 3 अशुद्धियाँ, का संग्रह 9 इंद्रिय अंग, 16 टेंडन, 16 प्लेक्सस, मांसपेशियों के 6 गुच्छे, 4 मांसपेशी रज्जु, 7 (रेशेदार) टांके, 14 हड्डी परिसर, 14 टर्मिनल गठन, 22 केशिकाएं, और 2 आंतें।" उस युग की शायद ही किसी पुस्तक में इतना विवरण दिया गया हो। ये शरीर में कैसे विकसित होते हैं, इसकी व्याख्या सुश्रुत संहिता में भी की गई है, जो एक दुर्लभ व्याख्या प्रस्तुत करती है।

यदि भारत का प्राचीन क्षेत्र चिकित्सा और शल्य चिकित्सा में अपनी प्रगति के लिए जाना जाता था, तो इसने दंत चिकित्सा में भी प्रगति के साधन विकसित किए हैं।

डॉ. आर्थर सेल्विन-ब्राउन द फिजिशियन्स थ्रू द एजेस (पेज 274) में लिखते हैं: "आपको यह जानकर आश्चर्य होगा कि दंत चिकित्सा अपनी सभी शाखाओं में प्रसिद्ध थी और पुराने हिंदू डॉक्टरों द्वारा इसका अभ्यास किया जाता था। आयुर्वेद में खोज करने पर, कोई पाता है कि मुख गुहा को समर्पित एक पूरा अध्याय है, जिसमें उन सभी ऑपरेशनों का वर्णन किया गया है जो वर्तमान पश्चिमी दंत चिकित्सा के लिए जाने जाते हैं। प्रारंभिक भारत में चिकित्सा

के प्रारंभिक विकास के बाद, यह अन्यत्र फैलना शुरू हुआ और तिब्बत में ही इसे सबसे अधिक लोकप्रियता मिली।

8वीं शताब्दी में यहीं पर चार भागों में एक बड़ा काम, तिब्बती में चतुतंत्र, जिसका नाम अमृतहृदय था, का संस्कृत से तिब्बती में अनुवाद किया गया था। इसके भीतर की शिक्षा बुद्ध भैषज्यगुरु को सौंपी गई थी। लेकिन कुछ अंश स्पष्ट रूप से चरक या सुश्रुत संहिता के उद्धरण हैं। इसके बाद यह कार्य मंगोलिया और फिर अगली शताब्दियों में रूस में चला गया।

कपड़ा

विल डुरैंट बताते हैं, «भारत में कपास की खेती अन्य जगहों की तुलना में पहले दिखाई देती है, मोहनजोदड़ो में इसका इस्तेमाल कपड़े के लिए किया जाता था।» यूसीएलए में इतिहास के प्रोफेसर डॉ. स्टैनली वोल्पर्ट ने अपनी पुस्तक इंडिया में लिखा है: «प्राचीन भारतीय पहले इंसान थे जिन्होंने सूती कातकर कपड़ा बनाया, जो हमें गर्मियों में सबसे आरामदायक पोशाक प्रदान करता है।»

अंततः कपास इंग्लैंड तक कैसे फैली, इसका वर्णन इस प्रकार किया जा सकता है: यह पहली शताब्दी की बात है जब अरब व्यापारी भारत से मलमल और केलिको के बढ़िया कपड़े लाते थे और इसे इटली और स्पेन को बेचते थे। मध्ययुगीन अरबों ने भारत से वस्त्र कला को अपनाया और उनके शब्द क़ुतन ने अंग्रेजी शब्द कॉटन दिया। शब्द क़ुतन मूल संस्कृत शब्द «कात» से लिया गया है, जिसका अर्थ है कपास की गेंद से धागा बनाना।

चरखे का आविष्कार संभवतः भारत में हुआ था, हालाँकि इसकी उत्पत्ति स्पष्ट नहीं है। यह मध्य युग में मध्य पूर्व से होते हुए यूरोप पहुंचा। क्वींसलैंड विश्वविद्यालय, ऑस्ट्रेलिया के

प्रोफेसर डी. पी. सिंघल ने अपनी पुस्तक भारत और विश्व सभ्यता (पृष्ठ 176) में लिखा है: «चरखा एक भारतीय आविष्कार है।»

भारत में प्राचीन काल से, कम से कम 4000 से 5000 साल पहले, कपास की खेती की जाती थी, फिर इसे धागे में पिरोया जाता था और कपड़े में बुना जाता था। यूनानियों को कपास के बारे में तब तक पता नहीं था जब तक सिकंदर ने भारत पर शासन नहीं किया था, जहां उन्हें पहली बार कपास मिली थी। उन्हें यह मिस्र, मेसोपोटामिया या फारस सहित उन पिछले देशों में नहीं मिला जहां से उन्होंने यात्रा की थी। इससे पहले, यूनानियों ने अपने बुने हुए कपड़ों में केवल ऊन का उपयोग किया था।

जब 17वीं शताब्दी में फ्रांसीसी यात्री और व्यापारी टेवर्नियर ने भारत का दौरा किया, तो उन्होंने सूती कपड़ों का वर्णन करते हुए कहा, «वे इतने हल्के और सुंदर हैं कि आप उन्हें अपने हाथों से महसूस भी नहीं कर सकते हैं, और नाजुक कढ़ाई मुश्किल से दिखाई देती है।» एक अन्य स्थान पर वह लिखते हैं, "एक फ़ारसी राजदूत भारत से वापस गया और उसने अपने सुल्तान को एक नारियल उपहार में दिया। दरबारी इस छोटे से उपहार से आश्चर्यचकित रह गए। लेकिन इससे भी अधिक आश्चर्य की बात यह थी कि जब नारियल खोला गया, तो उसमें से 30 गज का रोल [डाका] मुलमुल [कपड़ा] निकला।»

नीले रंग के विभिन्न रंगों को रंगने के लिए इंडिगोफेरा टिनक्टोरिया पौधे से निकाली गई प्रसिद्ध डाई का उपयोग किया जाता था। 20वीं सदी की शुरुआत तक भारत में 1.6 मिलियन एकड़ भूमि पर नील की खेती आम थी। जर्मनी ने 1897 से व्यावसायिक पैमाने पर सस्ते औद्योगिक कच्चे माल से इस डाई का निर्माण शुरू किया और विश्व पर एकाधिकार प्राप्त कर लिया। इसने भारतीय नील उद्योग को व्यावहारिक रूप से ख़त्म कर दिया।

यह ध्यान रखना दिलचस्प है कि रोमन भारतीय वस्त्रों के बहुत बड़े प्रशंसक थे, इस हद तक कि भारतीय वस्त्र खरीदने के लिए रोम का अधिकांश सोना उसके खजाने के बक्से से लिया जाता था। प्रारंभिक रोम के इन सोने के सिक्कों में से कुछ दक्षिणी भारत के कई हिस्सों में पाए गए हैं।

धातुकर्म

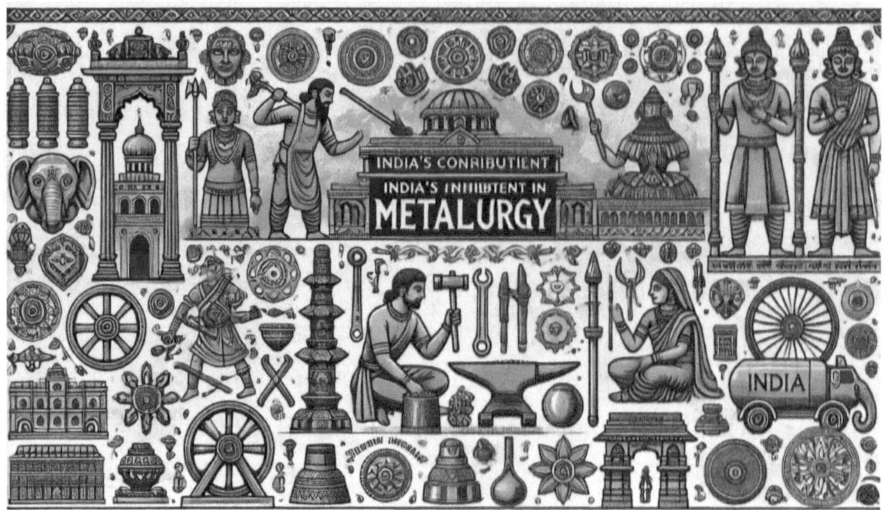

भारत में धातु के काम और धातुओं को गलाने और मिश्र धातु प्राप्त करने का एक महान इतिहास है, जो 3000 ईसा पूर्व में किया गया था। यह संकेत मिलता है कि भूमध्य सागर के लोगों के लिए स्टील के पहले हथियार भारत से आए थे।

44 पुराने ग्रंथ हैं जो भारतीय धातुकर्म की प्रक्रिया का वर्णन करते हैं। इनमें से सबसे प्रसिद्ध ग्रंथों में से एक को रसरत्न समुच्चय कहा जाता है। इसमें हमें इस प्रौद्योगिकी के कई पहलुओं, प्रयोगशाला, कोष्ठि यंत्र (भट्टी), तिर्यक पाटण यंत्र (रसायनों को रखने के बर्तन), ढेकी यंत्रम (आसवन बर्तन), और रासायनिक कार्य जैसी अन्य चीजों का विवरण मिलता है।

विल डुरैंट के अनुसार, «हिंदू सोने का खनन करने वाले पहले लोग हैं। मेगस्थनीज़ जैसे यूनानी आगंतुकों ने अपने अभिलेखों में इसका उल्लेख किया है। 5वीं शताब्दी ईसा पूर्व में फ़ारसी साम्राज्य में अधिकांश सोने का उपयोग भारत से आया था। भारत ने चांदी, तांबा, जस्ता, सीसा, टिन और लोहे का भी खनन किया।»

इस्पात बनाना

प्राचीन भारत का एक और प्रारंभिक विकास इसके कारीगरों की उच्च श्रेणी का स्टील बनाने की क्षमता है। एस. रामचंद्रन लौह एवं इस्पात प्रौद्योगिकी से संबंधित अपनी पुस्तक The Steel of India में लिखते हैं:

"इस्पात भारत में प्राचीन काल से जाना जाता है और वेदों में इसे अयस के रूप में संदर्भित किया गया है। पुरातात्विक प्रमाणों से पता चला है कि प्राचीन भारतीय इस्पात बनाने की कला जानते थे।"

जैसा कि फर्ग्यूसन ने अपनी पुस्तक A History of Indian and Eastern Architecture में उल्लेख किया है, "दिल्ली का लौह स्तंभ हमारी आंखें खोलता है कि हिंदू लोहे के स्तंभ को बनाने-वेल्ड करने में सक्षम हैं। किसी भी अन्य से बड़ा और बाद में यूरोप में भी इसकी नकल की गई। यह जानकर लगभग आश्चर्य होता है कि सदियों तक हवा और बारिश के संपर्क में रहने के बाद भी, इसमें जंग नहीं लगी है और लिखावट अब भी बहुत स्पष्ट है..."

तांबा एक और धातु थी जिसका उपयोग प्राचीन भारत के लोगों ने ठीक से करना सीखा था। 2000 ईसा पूर्व से ही, लोगों ने तांबे को सांचों में ढालकर तेज धार वाली बारीक तांबे की कुल्हाड़ियाँ बनाई थीं।

कांस्य 3000 ईसा पूर्व से पहले सिंधु घाटी क्षेत्र में जाना जाता था। कांस्य की वस्तुएं लुप्त मोम प्रणाली के माध्यम से बनाई जाती थीं, जिसका उपयोग आज भी किया जाता है।

जस्ता प्रौद्योगिकी के बारे में यूनानी ग्रंथों में उल्लेखों से पता चलता है कि ईसा पूर्व 6वीं या 5वीं शताब्दी में भारत से जस्ता वस्तुओं का व्यापार किया जाता था।

चरक ने सोने और चांदी की सुइयों को लेटने वाले कमरे के लिए आवश्यक चीजों के रूप में उल्लेख किया है। नवजात शिशु की नाभि काटने के लिए सोने या चांदी या लोहे के चाकू का सुझाव दिया गया। मनु-स्मृति में, लड़के के जन्म पर एक समारोह आयोजित किया जाता है, जिसमें नवजात शिशु को सुनहरे चम्मच से स्वाद के लिए थोड़ा शहद और घी का मिश्रण दिया जाता है।

टेम्परिंग स्टील को यूरोप के लिए अज्ञात भारत में पूर्णता तक लाया गया था। सिकंदर को भारतीय राजा से 30 पाउंड सोना नहीं बल्कि स्टील का अनमोल उपहार मिला।

भारत रंगाई, टैनिंग, साबुन बनाना, कांच और चीनी मिट्टी की चीज़ें, सीमेंट और धातुकर्म सहित कई रासायनिक और दवा उद्योगों में अग्रणी था। भारतीय कई तकनीकों में यूरोपीय विशेषज्ञों से कहीं आगे थे। दमिश्क स्टील के निर्माण का रहस्य अरबों ने फारसियों से और फारसियों ने भारत से लिया था।

चंदन का पेड़ भारत का मूल निवासी था। यह कर्नाटक है, जहां इसे उगाया जाता था और इसके सुगंधित गुणों के लिए इसका उपयोग किया जाता था। यह ग्रीस, अरब और

अन्य स्थानों पर निर्यात के लिए एक बेहतरीन उत्पाद बन गया। कस्तूरी एक और सुगंधित वस्तु थी जो नर कस्तूरी-हिरण की ग्रंथि से एकत्रित होकर मांग में आ गई थी। कपूर प्राचीन काल से भारत से निर्यात की जाने वाली एक और सुगंधित वस्तु थी, जिसका उपयोग अक्सर अनुष्ठानों और प्रार्थनाओं में किया जाता था।

वैदिक संस्कृति की कला में हीरे और कई अन्य कीमती और अर्ध-कीमती रत्नों का उपयोग किया जाता था। लेकिन यह विज्ञान केवल रत्नों का मूल्य कैसे जाना जाए और उन्हें सजावट के लिए कैसे उपयोग किया जाए, इसके बारे में ही नहीं था, बल्कि ज्योतिष में उनका उपयोग करने और ग्रहों के नकारात्मक प्रभाव को दूर करने या यहां तक कि उनकी सकारात्मक शक्तियों को बढ़ाने के लिए भी था। गरुड़ पुराण और अग्नि पुराण में इस प्रकार की बहुत सारी जानकारी है।

कृषि विकास

कृषि सदैव से भारत का आवश्यक व्यवसाय रहा है। ऋग और अथर्ववेद में कृषि को एक महान व्यवसाय माना गया था।

भारत पौधों की खेती के लिए सबसे पुराने क्षेत्रों में से एक था, जिसमें चावल, जूट, कपास, दालें, काली मिर्च, गेहूं, राई, अलसी, अखरोट और सेब, नाशपाती और आम जैसे फल शामिल थे। पुरातात्विक निष्कर्षों से पता चला है कि शीतकालीन अनाजों की कई प्रजातियाँ, जैसे कि जौ, जई और गेहूं, मसूर और चने जैसी फलियों के साथ, छठी सहस्राब्दी ईसा पूर्व से पहले उत्तर पश्चिम भारत में उगाए जाते थे।

अथर्ववेद ने पौधों को सात उप-भागों में विभाजित किया है, जैसे पेड़, घास, औषधि के लिए जड़ी-बूटियाँ, झाड़ियाँ, लताएँ, आदि। हमें महाभारत, विष्णु पुराण, मत्स्य पुराण आदि जैसे ग्रंथों में भी इनका उल्लेख मिलता है।

चरक ऋषि बताते हैं कि पेड़ों में भी अन्य प्राणियों की तरह जीवन होता है और भावनाएं भी होती हैं। यह उपयोग किए जाने वाले उपकरणों की सूची, फसलों की अधिक उपज के

लिए अच्छे कृषि प्रबंधन के तरीके, उपयोग किए जाने वाले उपकरण, संचालन, कटाई, वर्षा से निपटने, मवेशियों के प्रबंधन के साथ-साथ बीज संग्रह और भंडारण आदि पर सलाह देता है।

कृषि-पराशर और बृहत् संहिता भी मौसम के आधार पर जलवायु परिस्थितियों के साथ बुनियादी ज्योतिष का उपयोग करके बारिश की भविष्यवाणी करने के लिए सरल ज्योतिषीय मॉडल देने के लिए जाने जाते थे। उदाहरण के लिए, पराशर की पद्धति में चंद्रमा और सूर्य की स्थिति का उपयोग किया गया, जबकि वराहमिहिर (505-587 ई.पू.) की बृहत् संहिता में चंद्र की स्थिति पर विचार किया गया। इन विधियों का उपयोग अभी भी कई किसान करते हैं।

ऋग्वेद में गायों को बनाए रखने और खाने के लिए सही भोजन या चारा और पीने के लिए पानी के साथ उन्हें ठीक से प्रबंधित करने की प्रक्रिया भी शामिल है।

वृक्षायुर्वेद पराशर, जिसे ऋषि पराशर द्वारा रचा गया था, यह छह भागों में उन्नत वनस्पति विज्ञान का ज्ञान देता है। पराशर ऋषि ने पौधों की वृद्धि, विकास और देखभाल की पूरी प्रक्रिया को बहुत गहराई से जाना। वृक्षायुर्वेद पराशर के गहन अध्ययन में हमें बीज से वृक्ष बनने की प्रक्रिया का विस्तृत वर्णन मिलता है। इसका मतलब यह है कि सर जे.सी. बोस द्वारा पौधों में जीवन की खोज कोई खोज नहीं थी, बल्कि जो वेद और प्राचीन भारत पहले से ही जानते थे, उसकी पुष्टि मात्र थी। वास्तव में, इसकी पुष्टि ऋग्वेद (10.97.21) और महाभारत (शांति पर्व, अध्याय 184) में भी की गई है। ये किताबें दुनिया के संसाधनों और पर्यावरण को बचाते हुए अच्छी खेती के व्यावहारिक तरीके सुझाती हैं। उस समय के किसान मिट्टी की उर्वरता बढ़ाने के लिए पहले से ही फसल चक्र का उपयोग कर रहे थे, और पंक्तियों में बुआई प्राचीन काल से ही ज्ञात थी।

हम यह भी पाते हैं कि गरुड़ पुराण और अग्नि पुराण पशु विकारों और पशुधन से निपटने के बारे में निर्देश देते हैं। आयुर्वेद में शालिहोत्र संहिता नामक एक अलग भाग है, जो घोड़ों के उपचार के लिए महत्वपूर्ण है। कुछ पशुचिकित्सकों के अनुसार यह पुस्तक घोड़ों के उपचार की आधुनिक पुस्तकों से भी बेहतर है।

राजस्थान के पश्चिमी रेगिस्तान में, जैसलमेर में, केंद्रीय किले में राजा का महल इस तरह से बनाया गया था कि इसमें गिरने वाली पानी की हर बूंद को इकट्ठा किया जाता था, जिसे बाद में उपयोग के लिए संग्रहीत किया जाता था। और हवा से आने वाली हवा को इकट्ठा करने के लिए रास्ते बनाए गए थे ताकि महल के हर हिस्से में ठंडा प्रभाव महसूस किया जा सके।

विष्णु पुराण और श्रीमद् भागवत महापुराण में भी कुओं और पानी की टंकियों की स्थापना के महत्व का वर्णन किया गया है। लेकिन एक बार बन जाने के बाद इन कुओं और

टैंकों की देखभाल राज्य या क्षेत्र के शासकों द्वारा की जाती थी। भरपूर पानी के बिना चावल की खेती नहीं की जा सकती, जिसके लिए सिंचाई मुख्य जरूरतों में से एक है। इसलिए प्राचीन भारत में सिंचाई के विकास के साथ, यह एक ऐसा स्थान बन गया जहाँ चावल आसानी से उगाया जा सकता था।

कश्यप ऋषि की कृषि-सूक्ति, 2000 साल पहले चावल की खेती की एक विधि का वर्णन करती है, जिसका आज भी पालन किया जाता है। इतिहासकारों का मानना है कि चावल की «इंडिका» किस्म को सबसे पहले हिमालय की तलहटी वाले क्षेत्र में पालतू बनाया गया था, जैसे कि उत्तरपूर्वी भारत में, जो बाद में उड़ीसा, बंगाल, बर्मा, थाईलैंड, लाओस, वियतनाम और दक्षिणी चीन तक फैल गया। आज भी चावल की सबसे अधिक खेती इन्हीं देशों में की जाती है। विश्व के कुल चावल उत्पादन में अभी भी एशियाई किसानों की हिस्सेदारी 92 प्रतिशत है।

कला एवं संगीत

भारतवर्ष में संगीत प्राचीन काल से ही जाना और समझा जाता था, और मंत्रों के जाप के लिए यह सामवेद का प्राथमिक आधार था। संगीत का ज्ञान रहता है और राग-रागनियों की संख्या असंख्य है।

मुख्य भारतीय संगीत वाद्ययंत्र सरोद, वीणा, सारंगी, तम्बोरा, हारमोनियम, घाट, तबला, सितार आदि थे। ये वाद्ययंत्र सरल नहीं थे, बल्कि इन्हें बनाने के लिए विशेष सामग्री, शिल्प कौशल और प्रक्रियाओं के साथ-साथ वर्षों के कठिन अभ्यास की आवश्यकता होती थी। उन पर महारत हासिल करें।

यजुर्वेद के समय तक, विभिन्न प्रकार के पेशेवर संगीतकार सामने आ चुके थे, जैसे बांसुरी वादक, ढोल वादक, बांसुरी वादक और शंख बजाने वाले।

इस प्रकार, भारतीयों द्वारा बहुत प्रारंभिक युग में संगीत की खेती की गई थी, जैसे कि सात स्वरों के नाम (क्रम में) - सा (षड्ज), रे (ऋषभ), गा (गांधार), मा (मध्यम), पा (पंचम), ध (धैवत), नि (निषाद), सामवेद में और उनके वर्तमान क्रम में आते हैं।

सप्तक का अर्थ है कि आठवां स्वर सप्तक के पहले स्वर के समान है, लेकिन अगले उच्च स्तर का है। भारतीय सप्त-स्वर (सात स्वर) और पश्चिमी सप्तक इस प्रकार हैं:

- भारतीय सप्त-स्वर: सा, रे, गा, मा, पा, ध, नी, सा
- पश्चिमी सप्तक: दो, रे, मी, फा, सो, ला, ती, दो

भारतीय परंपरा में साहित्य और संगीत अविभाज्य हैं। विशेष मनोदशाओं और भावनाओं को पैदा करने के लिए कई रागों और रागिनियों को दिन या रात के विभिन्न समय, या वर्ष के मौसमों के लिए निर्दिष्ट किया जाता है।

छह प्रमुख रागों में शामिल हैं:

- बसंत: श्रोताओं के मन में बसंत की मिठास और ताजगी लाता है।
- श्री राग: जिसमें शाम की शांति और मौन है।
- मेघ मल्लार: जो आने वाले तूफान और बारिश का मूड लाता है।
- दीपक: निकट आती मृत्यु के दीपक जलाने के लिए, या यहां तक कि गायक के शरीर को आग की लपटों में जलाने के लिए बुलाया गया था, जिससे वह मर जाता है (कोई आश्चर्य नहीं कि यह अब शायद ही ज्ञात हो)।
- भैरव: बहुत लोकप्रिय हैं और आने वाली सुबह के प्रभाव और नए दिन की ताजगी और पक्षियों के गायन की याद दिलाते हैं।
- मल्कोस: जो सक्रियता की भावना पैदा करता है।

मुहम्मदियों के अधीन हिंदू संगीत लुप्त होने लगा। इस प्रकार, नृत्य और संगीत एक ठहराव पर आ गया, क्योंकि मुसलमानों द्वारा इस पर प्रतिबंध लगा दिया गया था। हालाँकि, खुद को बचाने के लिए, कई हिंदू संगीतकारों ने इस्लाम अपना लिया।

इसलिए, हम फिर से सामान्य ज्ञान का दृष्टिकोण पाते हैं कि भारत में अधिकांश मुसलमान हिंदू या पारिवारिक वंश से आते हैं। इस प्रकार, कई इस्लामी संगीतकार संगीत की वैदिक प्रणाली से निकले हुए हैं।

वैदिक नृत्य

कला की तरह, भारत में नृत्य केवल एक कलाकार की भावनात्मक मानसिकता या कल्पना की अभिव्यक्ति नहीं था, बल्कि उच्च आध्यात्मिक सिद्धांतों की व्याख्या थी। वास्तव में, वैदिक देवताओं में भगवान शिव को नर्तकों के राजा नटराज के रूप में जाना जाता है। उनका नृत्य ब्रह्मांड में फैली ऊर्जा की लय और मायावी (कल्पना) ऊर्जा के विनाश पर आधारित था, जिसके द्वारा सभी आत्माओं को मुक्ति (मोक्ष) प्राप्त करने के लिए भ्रम से मुक्त होने का अवसर दिया जाता है।

भरत मुनि ने अपना नाट्यशास्त्र लिखा, जिसमें उन्होंने बताया कि यह भगवान ब्रह्मा थे, जो सार्वभौमिक सृष्टि के द्वितीयक इंजीनियर थे, जिन्होंने लाखों साल पहले पृथ्वी ग्रह के लोगों के लिए नृत्य (नाट्य) और नाटक लाया था, पृथ्वी के अस्तित्व में आने के तुरंत बाद। रंजनी सहगल बताती हैं कि ऐसा कैसे हुआ होगा: "एक बार देवी-देवताओं ने भगवान ब्रह्मा से एक और वेद बनाने का अनुरोध किया, जिसे आम आदमी के लिए समझना आसान हो,

जो कि कलियुग में विशेष रूप से महत्वपूर्ण है। उनकी इच्छा को पूरा करते हुए, भगवान ब्रह्मा ने पंचम-वेद, पाँचवें वेद, या नाट्यवेद की रचना की।

ब्रह्मा ने ऋग्वेद से पथ्य (शब्द), यजुर्वेद से अभिनय (शरीर की गतिविधियों के संचारी तत्व, या माइम), सामवेद से गीत (संगीत और मंत्र), और रस (महत्वपूर्ण भावना और भावनात्मक भावना और अभिव्यक्ति) को लिया। अथर्ववेद से पांचवां वेद, नाट्यवेद बना। इस वेद की रचना करने के बाद, भगवान ब्रह्मा ने इसे ऋषि भरत को सौंप दिया और उनसे इसे पृथ्वी पर फैलाने के लिए कहा। इसका पालन करते हुए ऋषि भरत ने नाट्यशास्त्र पर ध्यान दिया। भरत ने गंधर्वों (स्वर्गदूतों) और अप्सराओं (स्वर्गीय नृत्य करने वाली लड़कियों) के समूहों के साथ मिलकर भगवान शिव के सामने नाट्य, नृत्य और नृत्य किया। यह भी संभव है कि भरतनाट्यम शब्द का नाम आंशिक रूप से ऋषि भरत के नाम पर पड़ा हो।

दक्षिण भारत के चिदम्बरम मंदिरों की दीवारों पर 108 मुद्राएँ अंकित हैं। कई नृत्य तकनीकें नाट्यशास्त्र से ली गई हैं, जैसे भरतनाट्यम, कुचिपुड़ी, कथक, कथकली, ओडिसी, मोहिनीअट्टम, कृष्णा अट्टम, भागवत मेला, मणिपुरी, आदि। ये भी महाकाव्यों पर आधारित कहानियों को कहने के विभिन्न तरीकों से विकसित हुए हैं, जैसे महाभारत, रामायण, या पंचतंत्र, हितोपदेश, या भागवत पुराण से कृष्णलीला, या अन्य पुराणों की कहानियाँ।

प्राचीन भारतीय शास्त्रीय नृत्य बहुत प्रभावशाली था। आजकल भारतीय नृत्य की यह प्राचीन कला व्यापक दर्शकों का आनंद ले रही है और अंतर्राष्ट्रीय मंच पर एक आवश्यक स्थान प्राप्त कर रही है। वैदिक परंपरा में कला कभी भी किसी कलाकार की कल्पना का प्रतिनिधित्व मात्र नहीं थी। यह हमेशा सत्य और सिद्धांतों, वास्तविकता के स्तरों को व्यक्त करने का एक सुंदर तरीका था जो हमारे निर्णय की भावना से परे मौजूद हो सकते हैं। यह हमेशा शुद्ध और सच्चा था।

प्राचीन काल में, कला और चित्रकला आध्यात्मिक ऊर्जा प्रदान करती थी। इस प्रकार, पेंटिंग या प्रतीक आध्यात्मिक सार का द्वार बन जाता है। दर्शन का अर्थ केवल ईश्वर को देखना ही नहीं है, बल्कि यह ईश्वर को देखने और देखे जाने के आदान-प्रदान में प्रवेश करना भी है।

ब्रिटिश शोधकर्ता श्री ग्रिफ़िथ कहते हैं, "अजंता में चित्र बनाने वाले कलाकार रचना जगत के सर्वोच्च व्यक्ति थे। यहां तक कि अजंता की दीवारों पर आसान ब्रश-स्ट्रोक से खींची गई सीधी खड़ी रेखाएं भी अद्भुत हैं।"

समुद्री मार्गों का ज्ञान

ऋग्वेद (1.25.7) में बताया गया है कि कैसे वरुण को उन सभी समुद्री मार्गों का पूरा ज्ञान था जिनका अनुसरण जहाजों द्वारा किया जाता था। ऋग्वेद (2.48.3) में यह भी उल्लेख है कि भारतीय व्यापारी विदेशी व्यापार के लिए जहाज भी भेजते थे।

रामायण और महाभारत जैसे महाकाव्यों में जहाजों और समुद्री यात्रा का उल्लेख है, और पुराणों में मत्स्य, वराह और मार्कंडेय पुराण में भी समुद्री यात्राओं की कहानियाँ हैं। रामायण के किष्किंधा कांड में, सुग्रीव वानर नेताओं को सीता की खोज के लिए समुद्र के द्वीपों में स्थित शहरों और पहाड़ों पर जाने के निर्देश देते हैं। रामायण में यह भी बताया गया है कि कैसे व्यापारी समुद्र पार यात्रा करते थे और राजाओं के लिए उपहार लाते थे।

महाभारत में, पर्व में यह वर्णन किया गया है कि कैसे द्रौपदी के पुत्रों ने अपने मामाओं को रथ उपलब्ध कराकर उनकी रक्षा की। एक अन्य पाठ बताता है कि कैसे पांडव गुप्त रूप से और विशेष रूप से निर्मित जहाज की मदद से उनके लिए योजनाबद्ध विनाश

से बच गए। यह जहाज बड़ा था, और मशीनरी और युद्ध के सभी प्रकार के हथियारों से सुसज्जित था, और तूफानों और लहरों का सामना करने में सक्षम था।

5वीं शताब्दी के वराहमिहिर द्वारा रचित बृहत् संहिता और 11वीं शताब्दी के नरपति राजा भोज द्वारा रचित संस्कृत पाठ युक्ति कल्पतरु में जहाजों के वर्गीकरण, आकार और सामग्रियों के बारे में जानकारी दी गई है, जिनसे उनका निर्माण किया गया था और उनके निर्माण की प्रक्रिया का उल्लेख है। यह यात्रियों के आराम के लिए, या सामान, जानवरों, या शाही कलाकृतियों के परिवहन के लिए जहाज को कैसे सुसज्जित किया जाए, इसके बारे में भी अधिक विवरण देता है। तीन अलग-अलग आकार के जहाज सर्वमंदिर, मध्यममंदिर और अग्रमंदिर थे।

प्राचीन भारतीयों ने न केवल व्यापार के उद्देश्य से, बल्कि अपनी संस्कृति को विकसित करने के लिए भी दुनिया के विभिन्न हिस्सों की यात्रा की। इस प्रकार वैदिक प्रभाव विश्व भर में फैल गया। ऐसा प्रतीत होता है कि 2540 ईसा पूर्व के आसपास उस बंदरगाह से मिस्र जैसे देशों के साथ व्यापार किया जाता था।

1292 ई. में, जब मार्को पोलो भारत आए, तो उन्होंने भारतीय जहाजों को "देवदार की लकड़ी से निर्मित, तख्तों से ढके, लोहे की कीलों से सीलबंद" बताया। दरारें एक विशेष प्रकार के गोंद से भरी हुई थीं। ये जहाज़ इतने विशाल थे कि इन्हें चलाने के लिए लगभग 300 नाविकों की आवश्यकता होती थी। उनके पास लोगों के रहने के लिए कई छोटे-छोटे कमरे थे। इन कमरों में हर तरह के आराम की व्यवस्था थी। फिर जब तली या आधार खराब होने लगता तो उस पर नई परत चढ़ा दी जाती। कभी-कभी, एक नाव में छह परतें भी होती थीं, एक के ऊपर एक।"

निकोलो कोंटी नामक एक अन्य यात्री 15वीं शताब्दी में भारत आया था। उन्होंने लिखा: «भारतीय जहाज़ हमारे जहाज़ों से बहुत बड़े हैं। इनका आधार तीन तख्तों से इस प्रकार बनाया जाता है कि वे तूफानों का सामना कर सकें। कुछ जहाज़ इस तरह से बनाए जाते हैं कि अगर एक हिस्सा बेकार हो जाए तो बाकी हिस्से काम करते हैं।»

भारत का एक अन्य पर्यटक जिसका नाम बर्थम है, लिखता है: «लकड़ी के तख्ते इस तरह जुड़े हुए हैं कि पानी की एक बूंद भी उसमें से नहीं जा सकती। एंकर कभी-कभी भारी पत्थरों से बनाये जाते थे। ईरान से केप कोमोरिन (कन्याकुमारी) आने में जहाज को आठ दिन लगेंगे।»

वास्को डी गामा का उल्लेख इंग्लैण्ड के संग्रहालय में उपलब्ध उनकी डायरियों में है। वह लिखते हैं कि जब उनका जहाज़ अफ्रीका में ज़ांज़ीबार के पास आया तो उन्होंने अपने जहाज़ के आकार से तीन गुना बड़ा जहाज़ देखा। वह उस जहाज के मालिक से मिलने के लिए एक अफ्रीकी दुभाषिया को ले गया, जो चंदन नाम का एक गुजराती व्यापारी था, जो

मसालों के साथ भारत से देवदार की लकड़ी और सागौन लाता था और हीरे वापस कोचीन के बंदरगाह पर ले जाता था। जब वास्को डी गामा उनसे मिलने गए तो चंदन साधारण पोशाक (आउटफिट) में बैठे थे। जब व्यापारी ने वास्को से पूछा कि वह कहाँ जा रहा है, तो उसने कहा कि वह भारत भ्रमण के लिए जा रहा है। तो वास्को डी गामा उनका पीछा करते हुए भारत आ गये।

आगे के सबूतों से पता चलता है कि प्राचीन भारत में जहाजरानी प्राचीन काल में फोनीशियन, यहूदी, असीरियन, यूनानी और रोमन जैसे लोगों के बीच और हाल ही में मिस्र, रोमन, तुर्क, पुर्तगाली, डच और अंग्रेजी जैसे लोगों के बीच विश्व व्यापार संबंधों में अग्रणी थी।

एक और सबूत दिखाया गया है, जैसे कि 1994 में दिल्ली में समुद्री यात्रा पर एक सम्मेलन में प्रस्तुत किए गए कागजात, जो दिखाते हैं कि 2500 ईसा पूर्व में भारतीय कपास को दक्षिण और मध्य अमेरिका में कैसे निर्यात किया गया था। एक अन्य रिपोर्ट से पता चलता है कि भारतीय कपास 4000 ईसा पूर्व, ऋग्वैदिक काल में, मैक्सिको तक पहुँच गया था।

साधारण तथ्य यह है कि भारत का समुद्री इतिहास पश्चिमी सभ्यता के जन्म से भी पहले का है। ऐसा माना जाता है कि दुनिया का पहला ज्वारीय गोदी 2300 ईसा पूर्व के आसपास हड़प्पा सभ्यता के दौरान लोथल में, गुजरात तट पर वर्तमान मांगरोल बंदरगाह के पास बनाया गया था। दूसरी सहस्राब्दी ईसा पूर्व से केरल का पश्चिमी एशिया और पूर्वी यूरोप के कई देशों के साथ समुद्री व्यापार था। इसके अलावा, भारतीय जहाज प्रशांत और हिंद महासागर में अन्य देशों के साथ व्यापार करते थे।

रोमन लेखक प्लिनी बताते हैं कि भारतीय व्यापारी कीमती पत्थर, खाल, कपड़े, मसाले, चंदन, इत्र, जड़ी-बूटियाँ, रेशम, कपास, चंदन, लकड़ी और विभिन्न प्रकार के निर्यात के बदले में रोम से बड़ी मात्रा में सोना ले जाते थे। अन्य भारतीय उत्पादों के। 844-848 ई. की अवधि में पश्चिमी क्षेत्रों से दैनिक राजस्व 200 मन (आठ टन) सोना होने का अनुमान लगाया गया था।

अंग्रेजों ने भारत के समुद्री उद्योग को कैसे खत्म किया?

भारतीय समुद्री शक्ति का पतन तेरहवीं शताब्दी में शुरू हुआ और जब पुर्तगाली भारत आये तो भारतीय समुद्री शक्ति लगभग लुप्त हो चुकी थी। बाद में उन्होंने व्यापार के लिए लाइसेंस और परमिट की एक प्रणाली शुरू की।

17वीं सदी तक यूरोपीय जहाज़ अधिकतम 600 टन के होते थे। लेकिन भारत में उन्होंने गोघा जैसे बड़े जहाज देखे, जो 1500 टन से भी ज्यादा के थे। जब पश्चिमी लोगों ने भारत से संपर्क किया तो वे उनके जहाजों को देखकर आश्चर्यचकित रह गये।

यूरोपीय कंपनियों ने इन जहाजों का उपयोग करना शुरू कर दिया और भारतीय कारीगरों से जहाज बनाने के लिए कई नए कारखाने खोले। 1811 में लेफ्टिनेंट वॉकर लिखते हैं, «अंग्रेजों के जहाजों की मरम्मत हर 12वें साल करनी पड़ती थी। लेकिन सागौन से बने भारतीय जहाज़ 50 वर्षों से भी अधिक समय से बिना किसी मरम्मत के काम कर रहे थे।» ईस्ट इंडिया कंपनी के पास दरिया दौलत नाम का जहाज था जो 87 साल तक बिना किसी मरम्मत के चलता रहा।

फ्रांसीसी यात्री वाल्ट्जर साल्विन्स ने 1811 में अपनी पुस्तक ले हिंदू में लिखा है, «हिंदू हमेशा जहाज निर्माण में आगे थे और आज भी वे यूरोपीय लोगों को एक या दो सबक सिखा सकते हैं। अंग्रेज़, जो कला सीखने में अच्छे थे, उन्होंने जहाज़ निर्माण के बारे में बहुत सी चीज़ें हिंदुओं से सीखीं।»

ब्रिटेन की शिपिंग कंपनियां जहाज निर्माण की भारतीय कला को बर्दाश्त नहीं कर सकीं और उन्होंने ईस्ट इंडिया कंपनी पर भारतीय जहाजों का उपयोग न करने के लिए दबाव डालना शुरू कर दिया। 1811 में, कर्नल वॉकर ने यह साबित करने के लिए डेटा दिया कि भारतीय जहाज़ बनाना बहुत सस्ता था। यदि ब्रिटिश बेड़े में केवल भारतीय जहाजों को शामिल किया जाए तो बड़ी बचत होगी। इससे ब्रिटिश जहाज निर्माता और व्यापारी परेशान हो गये।

लंदन बंदरगाह के कर्मचारी सबसे पहले मुद्दा बनाने और रोने वालों में से थे और उन्होंने कहा कि «हमारा सारा काम खत्म हो जाएगा।»

ईस्ट इंडिया कंपनी के निदेशक मंडल ने लिखा कि "भारतीय नाविकों के मन में यूरोपीय व्यवहार के प्रति जो भय और सम्मान था, वह सब ख़त्म हो गया जब उन्होंने यहाँ आने के बाद हमारा सामाजिक जीवन देखा। जब वे अपने देश लौटेंगे तो एशियाइयों के बीच हमारे बारे में बुरी बातें फैलाएंगे और हम अपनी श्रेष्ठता खो देंगे जो हानिकारक होगा।›

इस पर ब्रिटिश संसद ने सर रॉबर्ट पील की अध्यक्षता में एक समिति गठित की। "1814 में एक कानून पारित किया गया जिसके अनुसार भारतीयों ने ब्रिटिश नाविक बनने का अधिकार खो दिया और ब्रिटिश जहाजों पर कम से कम तीन-चौथाई ब्रिटिश नाविकों को नियुक्त करना अनिवार्य हो गया। जिस जहाज का मालिक ब्रिटिश नहीं होता था उसे लंदन बंदरगाह में प्रवेश की इजाजत नहीं थी और यह नियम बना दिया गया कि केवल इंग्लैंड में अंग्रेजों द्वारा बनाये गये जहाज ही इंग्लैंड में माल ला सकते थे। 1863 से इनका कड़ाई से पालन किया जाने लगा। भारतीय जहाजों में लाये जाने वाले माल पर कर बढ़ा दिया गया और उन्हें व्यापार से अलग करने का प्रयास किया गया। यह जहाज निर्माण की भारतीय कला के नष्ट होने की कहानी है।

प्राचीन भारत और अन्य देशों के बीच व्यापार न केवल समुद्री क्षमताओं के माध्यम से होता था, बल्कि चीन, तुर्किस्तान, फारस, बेबीलोन और मिस्र, ग्रीस और रोम तक फैले भूमि मार्गों के माध्यम से भी होता था, जो आगे भी बढ़ता रहा।

इन दिनों, भारत अभी भी जहाज निर्माण व्यवसाय में बहुत आगे है, ज्यादातर छोटे और मध्यम आकार के जहाजों में। अंग्रेजी शब्द नेविगेशन वास्तव में संस्कृत शब्द नवगति से आया है।

शिक्षा

भारत की प्रारंभिक शिक्षा व्यवस्था ग्राम आधारित थी। यह स्थानीय ऋषि और ब्राह्मण थे जो योग्य स्थानीय छात्रों को पढ़ाते थे। शिक्षा के स्थान को गुरुकुल या गुरु का स्थान कहा जाता था। ऋषि शिक्षक विद्यार्थियों के पिता समान होते थे। स्कूल का पहला आधार युवा छात्रों को सक्षम व्यक्तियों में बदलना था जो वैदिक धर्म के सिद्धांतों से अच्छी तरह परिचित हों, जो सम्माननीय और सम्माननीय होने की नींव हैं।

इसका उद्देश्य छात्रों में शारीरिक, नैतिक, बौद्धिक और आध्यात्मिक विकास के साथ-साथ चरित्र का निर्माण करना था, ताकि वे दुनिया में शांति के साथ आसानी से रह सकें। इतनी परिष्कृत शिक्षा शायद ही कहीं और पाई गई हो।

मुख्य विषय आत्मविद्या या स्वयं का ज्ञान था, जिसके बाद अन्य सभी विषयों का आसानी से अध्ययन किया जा सकता था। इसमें विज्ञान, कला और शिल्प, संगीत, ज्यामिति और बीजगणित जैसे गणित के साथ-साथ खगोल विज्ञान या ज्योतिष, तर्कशास्त्र, इतिहास,

कविता, व्याकरण और वैदिक ग्रंथों का ज्ञान शामिल था। कई स्कूलों ने सैनिकों को हथियार चलाने और घोड़ों और हाथियों को प्रशिक्षित करने का प्रशिक्षण दिया।

छात्रों तक ज्ञान पहुँचाने के तरीकों में शिक्षण और व्याख्यान, सस्वर पाठ, संवाद और फिर स्व-अध्ययन शामिल था। वेदों की प्राचीन शिक्षा को उपनिषदों के मार्गदर्शन से और अधिक विकसित किया गया, जिससे यह और अधिक परिष्कृत हुई।

इसके अलावा, ऐसी शिक्षा चरित्र निर्माण, अच्छी आदतें सीखने, जल्दी उठकर उचित दैनिक दिनचर्या का पालन करने, दैनिक अनुष्ठान करने और निश्चित रूप से सच बोलने और सरल जीवन जीने जैसे बुनियादी नैतिक मानकों को सीखने पर केंद्रित थी। कई वर्षों तक यह परंपरा लिखित शब्दों के बजाय मौखिक शिक्षाओं पर आधारित थी। क्योंकि शिक्षा केवल याद रखने से नहीं बल्कि अहसास से प्रदान की जाती थी, और शब्दों के कंपन में वर्णित ज्ञान की ऊर्जा पैदा करने के लिए ध्वनि का अपना महत्व था। इस तरह, छात्रों को मौखिक पाठ दिया जाता था जिस पर वे मनन करते, अध्ययन करते, सीखते और याद करते।

वैदिक परंपरा में, ज्ञान तीन बुनियादी चरणों द्वारा प्रदान या प्राप्त किया जा सकता है, जिसमें श्रवण (श्रवण), मनन (चिंतन) और निदिध्यासन (अहसास) शामिल हैं। इसका उद्देश्य समस्त मानवता के विकास के लिए वास्तविक शिक्षा और संस्कृति प्रदान करना था।

गुरु-शिक्षक के छात्र निःशुल्क शिक्षा के बदले शिक्षक के प्रति कर्तव्यों का पालन करेंगे। इसमें आश्रम की साफ-सफाई और रखरखाव में मदद करना, गायों को चराने में मदद करना या अनुष्ठानों में सहायता करना शामिल हो सकता है। हालाँकि, छात्र का प्राथमिक कर्तव्य अध्ययन करना और सीखना था। वैदिक शिक्षा सभी के लिए (प्रत्येक जाति और धर्म के लिए) निःशुल्क थी।

शिक्षा पूरी होने के बाद, गुरु या शिक्षक अंतिम निर्देश देंगे: «हमेशा सच बोलें, अपने कर्तव्यों का पालन करें। आचार्य को दक्षिणा देने के बाद पुरानी परंपराओं को न तोड़ें। धर्म को कभी मत छोड़ो। महान बनने का अवसर न चूकें। माँ को देवी मानो, पिता को भगवान मानो। आचार्य (शिक्षक) को भगवान (देव) के समान मानें। अतिथि (अतिथि) को भगवान (देव) के समान समझो। अच्छे कर्म करो। आप जो भी उपहार दें, पूरे प्यार और सम्मान के साथ दें।

"यदि तुम्हारे मन में धर्म या सदाचार के संबंध में कोई संदेह उत्पन्न हो, तो जो श्रेष्ठ और कोमल हृदय वाले ब्राह्मण हों, उनसे सलाह लो और जैसा वे कहें, वैसा ही करो। यह मेरा तुम्हें निर्देश है, तुम इसका पालन करो।"

पंजाब और हरियाणा उच्च न्यायालय के सेवानिवृत्त मुख्य न्यायाधीश एम. रामा जोइस ने 2010 में लेखक से कहा था, «यह वास्तव में देश को हमारे द्वारा देखे गए सभी भ्रष्टाचार

से छुटकारा दिलाने का सबसे अच्छा तरीका था।» उन्होंने कहा कि स्वतंत्रता-पूर्व समय के दौरान, बच्चे महाभारत और रामायण या पुराणों जैसे महान महाकाव्यों से धर्म के उदाहरण और उन महान नायकों के बारे में सुनते थे जिन्होंने धर्म के नियमों के तहत विभिन्न स्थितियों में कार्य किया था। इसलिए, पढ़ने और लिखने से पहले बच्चों को उचित चरित्र के बारे में शिक्षित किया गया और यह बताया गया कि एक उचित इंसान के रूप में कैसे कार्य किया जाए, जीवन की विभिन्न परिस्थितियों में क्या सही है या क्या गलत है, इसका निर्णय कैसे किया जाए। दुर्भाग्य से, यह 1947 के बाद हुआ जब स्वतंत्र भारत के नए प्रशासन ने निर्णय लिया कि धर्म के सिद्धांतों को सीखना धार्मिक अध्ययन था, और नई सरकार अब ऐसे प्री-स्कूलों का समर्थन नहीं कर सकती है।

इस प्रकार, धर्म के तहत ऐसे सभी सिद्धांत अब भारत के स्कूलों में नहीं पढ़ाए जाएंगे। जैसा कि एम. रामा जोइस ने अपनी पुस्तक धर्म: द ग्लोबल एथिक में बताया है, «हमारी सभी वर्तमान समस्याएं भौतिकवादी शिक्षा के प्रभाव में, धर्म शिक्षा से असहमत होने का प्रत्यक्ष परिणाम हैं।» धर्म का कोई विकल्प नहीं है। यह शाश्वत सत्य है।

महाभारत (शांति पर्व, 90.3) में भी कहा गया है कि, «राजा या किसी भी शासक का उचित कार्य या राजनीतिज्ञ धर्म के अनुसार शासन करना है न कि जीवन की विलासिता का आनंद लेना।» इस प्रकार, एक राजनेता को अपने पद का लाभ उठाने के लिए नहीं, बल्कि धर्म के नियमों के मार्गदर्शन में लोगों के लाभ को ध्यान में रखते हुए अपने कर्तव्यों का पालन करना होता है।

मनु-संहिता (10.63) में बताए गए धर्म के मूल नियम हैं:
* अहिंसा (अहिंसा),
* सत्य (सच्चाई),
* अस्तेय (अवैध धन अर्जित न करना),
* शौच (शुद्धता), और
* इंद्रियनिग्रह (इंद्रियों पर नियंत्रण)।

जब इस प्रकार का प्रशिक्षण कम उम्र में प्राप्त हो जाता है, तो यह जीवन भर चल सकता है। धर्म के सिद्धांत कोई क्षेत्रीय या धार्मिक प्रशिक्षण नहीं है, बल्कि यह एक धर्मनिरपेक्ष प्रशिक्षण है। धर्म अक्सर बांटता है, जबकि धर्म सभी को समान रूप से देखकर जोड़ता है। धर्म को सभी मनुष्यों पर लागू किया जा सकता है। इस प्रकार, यह समाज में सद्भाव बनाए रखता है और टकराव पैदा नहीं करता।

कहा जाता है कि नालंदा विश्वविद्यालय में बहुत सारे छात्र और शिक्षक थे। इसे शुरुआत में एक छोटे से गाँव में बनाया गया था, लेकिन यह एक विकासशील शहर और बौद्ध शिक्षण केंद्र बन गया। भगवान बुद्ध ने प्रवारिक वन में और राजगीर में रहकर यहां कई व्याख्यान दिये थे। यह वेदांत, सांख्य और ज्योतिष सिखाने के लिए जाना जाता था।

कुछ धार्मिक संघर्षों के कारण, अन्य समुदायों ने भारतीयों को अपनी संस्कृति के प्रति कम आकर्षित और कम भरोसा करने के लिए यथासंभव अधिक से अधिक वैदिक पुस्तकों को नष्ट करने का प्रयास किया।

वैदिक अर्थशास्त्र

प्राचीन भारतीय अर्थव्यवस्था मुख्यतः स्थानीय, गाँव-आधारित अर्थव्यवस्था थी। वैदिक समझ का पहला सिद्धांत यह है कि हम हर चीज़ को सर्वोच्च सत्ता की ऊर्जा के रूप में देखते हैं।

ऐसे व्यापार करने से जो जानबूझकर दूसरों को धोखा दे, हमारे दिल और विचार कठोर हो जाएंगे और हम सभी जीवित प्राणियों और यहां तक कि खुद में भी दिव्य सौंदर्य की खोज करने में असमर्थ हो जाएंगे। व्यापार में ईमानदारी होनी चाहिए और प्राचीन भारत इस प्रकार के व्यवसाय में था। बेईमानी और धोखाधड़ी से कमाया गया त्वरित मुनाफा निश्चित रूप से हमें नीचे गिरा देगा। व्यवसाय को धार्मिक सिद्धांतों की नींव पर रखा जाना चाहिए।

आजकल, हमने देखा है कि जिन कंपनियों के पास ताकत है और जिनका मकसद भारी मुनाफा कमाना है, वे विभिन्न खाद्य पदार्थ, दवाएं, पेय पदार्थ आदि का उत्पादन करती हैं, जिनके बारे में कहा जाता है कि ये बिना किसी दुष्प्रभाव के स्वास्थ्य के लिए बहुत

फायदेमंद होते हैं। समय-समय पर, हमने सीखा है कि इस प्रकार के उत्पाद वास्तव में जनता पर थोपे गए हैं जिनके हानिकारक दुष्प्रभाव हुए हैं।

हालाँकि, हमें हमेशा यह ध्यान रखना चाहिए कि किसी कंपनी की ओर से एक तथ्य के रूप में प्रस्तुत की गई कहानी जिसका उद्देश्य सत्ता, नियंत्रण या मुनाफा है, आमतौर पर ऐसी कहानी होती है जिस पर भरोसा नहीं किया जाना चाहिए। प्राचीन भारत वैदिक काल में ऐसे मामलों से पूरी तरह परहेज करता था।

गाँव और कस्बे तथा उनकी स्थानीय अर्थव्यवस्था तब विकसित होगी जब प्रचुर मात्रा में अनाज, सब्जियाँ, जड़ी-बूटियाँ, फलों से भरे पेड़, ताजे और साफ पानी से बहने वाली नदियाँ और खनिजों से भरी पहाड़ियाँ होंगी। इस स्थिति में, सभी के लिए बहुत कुछ होगा। यदि समाज के पास इस तरह से पर्याप्त प्राकृतिक संसाधन हैं, तो उसे विशाल औद्योगिक परिसरों का चयन क्यों करना चाहिए, जिनके लिए पुरुषों के श्रम की आवश्यकता होती है, उन्हें अंधेरे कारखानों में भेजा जाता है, जहां वे डॉलर के बदले में अपना जीवन व्यतीत करते हैं, और फिर उन्हें अपने हिस्से का एक हिस्सा देना पड़ता है। सरकारी करों के लिए कमाई?

समाज जितना अधिक कृत्रिम आवश्यकताओं पर निर्भर होता है यह उतना ही असुरक्षित होता है। इस प्रकार, जब भी पर्याप्त तेल, गैस, बिजली न होने का डर होता है, या जब ऐसी आधुनिक वस्तुओं की कीमतें बहुत अधिक हो जाती हैं, तो सभ्यता को नुकसान होता है और अर्थव्यवस्था धीमी हो जाती है। अब हम उन पर इतने निर्भर हो गए हैं कि हमें लगता है कि उनके बिना हम जीवित नहीं रह सकते। इस प्रकार, लोग अधिक भौतिकवादी चीजें खरीदने के लिए संघर्ष करने और अधिक पैसा कमाने के लिए बाध्य हैं। इस तरह, वे एक ऐसी व्यवस्था से बंधे हैं जिसका लक्ष्य समाज को वास्तविक लाभ प्रदान करने या संतुलित अर्थव्यवस्था में रहने के बजाय मुनाफा है।

आज की आर्थिक व्यवस्था आपको नियंत्रण में रखती है, आपके द्वारा भुगतान किए जाने वाले बिलों में व्यस्त रहती है। आपको एक ऐसी प्रणाली के लिए मजबूर किया जाता है जिसमें आप जीवन की बुनियादी जरूरतों के लिए भुगतान करने के लिए सर्वशक्तिमान डॉलर के लिए काम करते हैं। और आपको अक्सर उस व्यवसाय या उद्योग में दूसरों के लाभ के लिए काम करने के लिए मजबूर किया जाता है जो आपको काम पर रखेगा।

भले ही आप अपने खुद के बॉस हों या डॉक्टर या वकील जैसे पेशेवर हों, आपको लाइसेंस प्राप्त करना होगा और अपना लाइसेंस खोने के डर से सिस्टम के भीतर काम करना होगा। दूसरे शब्दों में, आपको उच्च स्तर के दार्शनिक विचार, आत्म विकास या आध्यात्मिक अभ्यास के बारे में सोचने का समय सीमित है, क्योंकि आपको यह सुनिश्चित करना होगा कि आपके पास आज के जीवन में आपकी ज़रूरत की हर चीज़ के लिए भुगतान करने के लिए पैसा है।

बहुत से लोग इतने डरे हुए हैं कि वे नौकरी नहीं बदल सकते (उन्हें पसंद नहीं है) सिर्फ इसलिए क्योंकि नौकरी उन्हें अपने सभी बिलों का भुगतान करने और अपने जीवन में कुछ संतुलन बनाए रखने की अनुमति देती है। यह अधिकांश लोगों के लिए आज की आर्थिक व्यवस्था की प्रकृति है। यही कारण है कि आज कई लोगों को दो या तीन नौकरियां करनी पड़ती हैं। इस तरह की जीवनशैली में बहुत तनाव होता है और कुछ लोग निराशाजनक व्यवहार करने लगते हैं, जिससे अपराध में वृद्धि होती है। यह लोगों को आध्यात्मिक क्षमता और सामाजिक विकास से दूर रखता है और इसलिए समाज ईश्वरविहीन और अव्यवस्थित हो जाता है। यह मानव अस्तित्व का बिल्कुल भी उद्देश्य नहीं है।

वैदिक व्यवस्था लोगों को अनावश्यक आवश्यकताओं के लिए काम करने के इस चक्र से मुक्त करने के लिए थी। यह आपको अपने आध्यात्मिक और सामाजिक विकास तक पहुंचने के लिए समय और ऊर्जा रखते हुए अपनी बुनियादी जरूरतों के लिए काम करने के लिए मुक्त करने के लिए थी। वैदिक अर्थव्यवस्था प्रणाली के अनुसार आर्थिक विकास का मूल सिद्धांत भूमि और उसकी उपज है। जो भूमि पर नियंत्रण रखता है वह भोजन पर नियंत्रण रखता है। जो भोजन और ईंधन को नियंत्रित करता है वह दुनिया को नियंत्रित करता है। इसीलिए ज़मीन हमेशा स्थानीय किसानों के हाथ में होनी चाहिए, ताकि सब कुछ साझा हो और सभी लोग विकास कर सकें।

इसके निष्कर्ष में, हमें यह समझना चाहिए कि इस दुनिया में प्रदूषण का सबसे बड़ा रूप पद, शक्ति और धन के लिए प्रतिस्पर्धा है। व्यवसाय करने के बेहतर तरीकों और अधिक गुणवत्ता वाले उत्पादों का उत्पादन करने पर काम करना स्वाभाविक है। जिसके पास सर्वश्रेष्ठ होगा वह सफल होगा। लेकिन ईर्ष्या, ईष्र्या और शक्ति पर या केवल अधिक पैसे के लिए आधारित प्रतिस्पर्धा, व्यक्तियों और कंपनियों को आगे बढ़ने, अधिक बाजार हिस्सेदारी, अधिक ग्राहक प्राप्त करने और अधिक सस्ते में उत्पाद बनाने के गलत तरीकों को स्वीकार करने के लिए मजबूर करती है। इस दुनिया को पैसे के शासक जहाज, गंदी राजनीति और झूठी और गुमराह अर्थव्यवस्था से शुद्ध करने के लिए एक नई प्रणाली का उदय होना चाहिए।

हमें ऐसा परिवर्तन करने के लिए पर्याप्त रूप से मजबूत होना होगा और फिर एक संतुलित और आध्यात्मिक रूप से विकसित समाज बनाने के लिए वैदिक धर्म के सिद्धांतों का उपयोग करना होगा।

सैन्य एवं मार्शल आर्ट

सैन्य विज्ञान का सबसे प्रारंभिक रूप धनुर्वेद नामक मानक वैदिक पाठ में वर्णित है। हथियारों का उपयोग और प्रशिक्षण सेना का सबसे महत्वपूर्ण हिस्सा था, जिसमें उन दिनों घोड़ों की सवारी करते समय धनुष और तीर का उपयोग शामिल था।

इसमें केवल एक तीर चलाना ही शामिल नहीं था बल्कि कई अन्य हथियारों पर कई तीर चलाना भी शामिल था। इनमें यन्त्रमुक्ता नामक फेंकी गई मिसाइलें शामिल थीं; हाथ से फेंके गए, हस्तमुक्ता; धारण किए जाने वाले हथियार, या मुक्तामुक्त, जैसे भाला, त्रिशूल, या तलवार, फिर प्राकृतिक हथियार जैसे मुट्ठी, उंगलियां, पैर, इत्यादि।

वैदिक आर्य बारूद के अवयवों, जैसे गंधक, लकड़ी का कोयला, शोरा, से अच्छी तरह परिचित थे और ये सभी स्थानीय स्तर पर आसानी से प्राप्त हो जाते थे। वास्तव में, यूनानी लेखकों ने हिंदुओं द्वारा उपयोग किए जाने वाले आग्नेयास्त्रों का वर्णन किया है। ऐसा प्रतीत होता है कि रॉकेट और तोपें अन्य क्षेत्रों में लोकप्रिय होने से पहले एक प्रारंभिक भारतीय आविष्कार थे।

ब्रह्मास्त्र एक अन्य हथियार था जिसका वैदिक ग्रंथों में बार-बार उल्लेख किया गया है। ये एक प्रकार के मंत्र हथियार थे जो तीरों से जुड़े होते थे जो अपने लक्ष्य पर उतरने या हिट होने पर परमाणु विस्फोट का प्रभाव पैदा करते थे, आज के परमाणु बमों की तरह नहीं जो क्षेत्र में सब कुछ नष्ट कर देते हैं।

भारत मार्शल आर्ट के अपने अनूठे रूप के लिए भी जाना जाता है, जो हजारों वर्षों से अस्तित्व में रहे सबसे शुरुआती विकासों में से एक है। वास्तव में, मार्शल आर्ट के कई रूप जो यहां से सामने आए हैं, उन्हें सबसे पहले भारत की तकनीकों द्वारा पेश किया गया था। भारत से मार्शल आर्ट की कुछ शैलियाँ बौद्ध धर्म के साथ तिब्बत, फिर चीन और बाद में जापान तक गईं।

भारत में मार्शल आर्ट को शस्त्रविद्या और धनुर्विद्या कहा जाता था। भागवत पुराण, विष्णु पुराण, महाभारत और अन्य ग्रंथों में व्यक्तिगत लड़ाई का वर्णन, इस्तेमाल किए गए हथियारों का वर्णन शामिल है, जिनमें पेड़, तलवारें, धनुष और तीर, चट्टानें, मुक्के आदि शामिल हैं।

यहां तक कि कथकली जैसी शैलियों की नृत्य चालें, जो केरल में भी प्रसिद्ध हैं, को मार्शल आर्ट में शामिल किया गया था। कलारीपयट् भारत में मार्शल आर्ट की एक प्रसिद्ध प्रणाली है, लेकिन ज्यादातर केरल मूल की है।

मार्शल आर्ट के सबसे पुराने रूपों में से एक लाठी या लंबी छड़ी है। इस कला का अभ्यास भारत में हजारों सालों से किया जा रहा है और यह आज भी कई ग्रामीण क्षेत्रों में प्रचलित है। लाठी का उपयोग आत्मरक्षा और युद्ध में किया जाता था, और यह आज भी कई मार्शल आर्ट स्कूलों में सिखाई जाती है।

प्राचीन भारतीय विमानों की अद्वितीय क्षमताएँ

इन विमानों में कुछ अद्वितीय क्षमताएँ थीं, जिनमें शामिल हैं:

- रूप बदलने की क्षमता: ये विमान अपने आकार को बदल सकते थे।
- अत्यंत बड़े या छोटे होने की क्षमता: ये विमान बहुत बड़े या बहुत छोटे हो सकते थे।
- बहुत भारी या भारहीन बनने की क्षमता: ये विमान अत्यधिक भारी या बिल्कुल भारहीन हो सकते थे।
- इच्छित वस्तु को प्राप्त करने की क्षमता: ये विमान किसी भी इच्छित वस्तु को सुरक्षित कर सकते थे।
- सभी इच्छाओं से मुक्त होने की क्षमता: ये विमान सभी इच्छाओं से मुक्त हो सकते थे।
- आकाश में उड़ने की क्षमता: ये विमान आकाश में उड़कर कहीं भी जा सकते थे।

यांत्रिक विमानों की आवश्यकता:

उस समय, इन विमानों की अद्वितीय क्षमताओं के कारण यांत्रिक उड़ान की आवश्यकता नहीं थी। इन विशेषताओं के कारण, वे अपनी इच्छाओं के अनुसार कहीं भी जा सकते थे और विभिन्न प्रकार की अद्वितीय शक्तियों का प्रदर्शन कर सकते थे।

प्राचीन भारतीय विमानों का विवरण

भगवान ब्रह्मा, जो ब्रह्मांड के मुख्य देवता और इंजीनियर माने जाते हैं, ने कुछ देवताओं के लिए कई विमानों का विकास किया था। ये विमान विभिन्न प्राकृतिक आकारों में थे और इनमें पंखों का उपयोग किया गया था, जैसे मोर, गरुड़, हंस आदि।

विमानों के प्रकार:

विमानों के तीन मुख्य प्रकार थे:

1. त्रेता युग: इस युग में लोग मंत्रों या शक्तिशाली स्तोत्रों में कुशल थे। इसलिए, इस युग के विमान मंत्रों के ज्ञान के माध्यम से संचालित होते थे।

2. द्वापर युग: इस युग में लोगों ने तंत्र या अनुष्ठान का पर्याप्त ज्ञान विकसित कर लिया था। अतः द्वापर युग के विमान तांत्रिक ज्ञान के उपयोग से संचालित होते थे।

3. कलियुग: इस युग के विमान कृत्रिम या यांत्रिक के रूप में जाने जाते हैं।

वेदिक निर्देश:

वेदिक ग्रंथ «समरांगण सूत्रधार» में ऐसे इंजनों को बनाने के निर्देश शामिल हैं, जिनमें प्रकाश के मैनुअल, वायुमार्ग, सामान्य और मजबूर लैंडिंग की प्रक्रियाएं, पायलटों की स्थिति के बारे में निर्देश, उड़ान के समय पहनने के लिए कपड़े, विमान के निर्माण के लिए धातु, बिजली आपूर्ति आदि शामिल हैं।

विशेषताएँ:

कुछ विमान न केवल आकाश में उड़ सकते हैं, बल्कि भूमि पर भी चल सकते हैं और समुद्र में डुबकी लगाकर पानी के भीतर यात्रा कर सकते हैं। डेविड चाइल्ड्रेस ने अपनी पुस्तक «विमाना एयरक्राफ्ट ऑफ़ एन्शिएंट इंडिया एंड एटलांटिस» में कई रिपोर्टें दी हैं, जो प्राचीन वेदिक ग्रंथों में वर्णित आकार और आकार के यूएफओ के साथ मुठभेड़ों के प्रत्यक्षदर्शी विवरणों का वर्णन करती हैं।

वैदिक पर्यावरणवाद

वैदिक पर्यावरणवाद

पर्यावरण की रक्षा के लिए कुछ गतिविधियाँ, चाहे जल संरक्षण की प्रणालियों के माध्यम से, नदियों और नहरों का विकास, और कृषि प्रणालियों के माध्यम से भूमि और वनों को बनाए रखना, प्राचीन भारत में दर्ज हैं।

पर्यावरण का अर्थ है प्रकृति, और यह किसकी प्रकृति है? यह भगवान का स्वभाव है। क्या इसे किसी और ने बनाया है? वास्तव में, मानव जाति अभी भी जटिलता वाले वातावरण की खोज करने की कोशिश कर रही है। हमारे सभी आविष्कारों में, हम जिन सामग्रियों और संसाधनों का उपयोग करते हैं, उनमें से अधिकांश ईश्वर द्वारा दिए गए हैं। और हमें इसके प्रति उचित सम्मान दिखाना चाहिए। यह सोचना कि हम हर चीज़ के मालिक हैं, भ्रम है। वास्तव में, जिस मस्तिष्क से हम सोचते हैं, वह हमारा बनाया हुआ नहीं बल्कि ईश्वर द्वारा दिया गया है।

पर्यावरण की परवाह न करने, हमारे प्राकृतिक संसाधनों का दुरुपयोग करने, भूमि और जंगलों का उचित प्रबंधन न करने के रूप में ग्रह के प्रति हिंसा, सभी प्रकार से ईश्वर के प्रति अनादर है और हमें कभी भी संसाधनों को बर्बाद नहीं करना चाहिए। हालाँकि, अगर जिन लोगों के पास कोई वास्तविक आध्यात्मिक समझ नहीं है, वे जो चाहें प्राप्त करने के लिए पृथ्वी का दुरुपयोग करना शुरू कर दें, तो संसाधनों की आपूर्ति कम होने लगती है और पृथ्वी, एक जीवित जीव होने के नाते, उत्पादन करना बंद कर देती है या समाज की ज़रूरतों का जवाब देना जैसा कि वह करता था।

पृथ्वी का सम्मान करने और उसके संसाधनों को साझा करने में सहयोग करने के बजाय, जब हम उन पर लड़ते हैं, तो यह धरती माता के लिए सबसे निराशाजनक होता है। तब कमी, सूखा और जंगल की आग होगी; धीरे-धीरे वस्तुओं की कीमतें बढ़ेंगी और अधिक लोग गरीब हो जाएंगे जिससे विश्व में गरीबी फैल जाएगी।

सम्यक दृष्टि एवं वैदिक समझ यह है कि प्रत्येक वस्तु परमात्मा की संपत्ति है। हम निश्चित रूप से जब यह शरीर छोड़ेंगे तो उन्हें अपने साथ नहीं ले जा सकते। किसी भी चीज़ का उपयोग करने का उचित तरीका भगवान की सेवा करना और पर्यावरण की देखभाल करना है।

व्यक्तिगत स्वतंत्रता और शासन के स्रोत के रूप में भारत

भारत के राष्ट्रपति ए.पी.जे. अब्दुल कलाम ने एक बार सही कहा था: «हमारे इतिहास के 3000 वर्षों में, दुनिया भर के लोगों ने आकर हम पर शासन किया, हमारी ज़मीनों और दिमागों पर कब्ज़ा कर लिया। सिकंदर के बाद से, यूनानी, तुर्क, मुग़ल, पुर्तगाली, अंग्रेज़, फ्रेंच, डच, ये सब आये और हमें लूटा और कब्ज़ा कर लिया। फिर भी हमने किसी अन्य राष्ट्र के साथ ऐसा नहीं किया है। हमने किसी भी देश की ज़मीन या इतिहास नहीं लिया है या लेने का प्रयास भी नहीं किया है, क्योंकि हम दूसरों की स्वतंत्रता का सम्मान करते हैं। यह वह स्वतंत्रता है जिसे वैदिक संस्कृति ने सदैव बढ़ावा दिया है।

आज भी भारत अधिक जनसंख्या वाला विश्व का सातवां सबसे बड़ा और दूसरा सबसे अधिक आबादी वाला देश है। एक संविधान, एक राष्ट्रीय निर्वाचित संसद इत्यादि, जो इसे सबसे बड़ा लोकतंत्र बनाती है।

इस विचारधारा में, डॉ. विल ने कहा, «आइए हम आगे याद रखें कि भारत हमारी जाति की मातृभूमि थी, और संस्कृत, यूरोप की भाषाओं की जननी; वह दर्शनशास्त्र की जननी थी; गणित की जननी; बुद्ध के माध्यम से माँ ईसाई धर्म में आदर्शों का; स्वशासन और लोकतंत्र के ग्राम समुदाय के माध्यम से माँ। भारत माता अंदर है कई मायनों में हम सभी की माँ।»

वैदिक सभ्यता में महान विचारक थे जिन्होंने कई अतिरिक्त राजनीतिक विचारों की उत्पत्ति में मदद की। उदाहरण के लिए, कौटिल्य, चाणक्य के नाम से लोकप्रिय पंडित ने अपने अर्थशास्त्र में ऐसे सिद्धांत स्थापित किए जिनका उपयोग आज भी संगठनों द्वारा किया जाता है, जैसे कि नाटो (उत्तर अटलांटिक संधि संगठन)।

महाभारत जैसे ग्रंथों में सरकार और राजा या शासक के कर्तव्यों के बारे में बहुत सारी जानकारी है। इसके अलावा, ये वैदिक सिद्धांत जो प्राचीन महाभारत और अन्य वैदिक पुस्तकों में पाए जाते हैं, किसी भी नेता के लिए लागू होते हैं, चाहे वे स्थानीय, राज्य या राष्ट्रीय हों।

किसी भी शासक को कोई भी प्राधिकारी पद लेने से पहले, एक उचित संविधान होना चाहिए जो वास्तविकता को स्पष्ट करे। सरकार और देश के शासक का उद्देश्य धर्म और उन सभी सत्य साधकों की रक्षा करना है जो इसका पालन करते हैं।

धर्म के सिद्धांत

धर्म का अर्थ है वह मार्ग जो व्यक्तिगत और सामाजिक रूप से सद्भाव लाने और बनाए रखने में मदद करता है, और सत्य जो हमें नकारात्मक विचारों से मुक्त कर सर्वोच्च वास्तविकता तक पहुंचा सकता है।

कहा गया है कि देश के संविधान का मुख्य उद्देश्य धर्म और धर्म की रक्षा करना होना चाहिए, धर्म के कानून के अनुसार प्रजा के बीच धार्मिकता को बनाए रखना।

संविधान को वैदिक ग्रंथों की समीक्षा के बाद ही लिखा जाना चाहिए, जिसमें आध्यात्मिकता का सार्वभौमिक मानक हो, जो समाज के विकास और उन्नति के लिए हो।

वैदिक मानकों में इसे रामराज्य कहा जाता है, क्योंकि उस समय के शासक, अर्थात् भगवान राम, ने सभी के लाभ के लिए काम किया और सभी ने मिल-जुलकर सहयोग किया।

संस्कृत भाषा में प्रजा के प्रधान रक्षक को क्षत्रिय कहा जाता है। इस शब्द का अर्थ योद्धा है, लेकिन मूलतः यह उस व्यक्ति को संदर्भित करता है जो लोगों को क्षति या दुःख से बचाता है, या जो समस्याओं और कठिनाइयों को दूर करता है।

सभी प्राणियों की रक्षा करना एक उचित क्षत्रिय का परम कर्तव्य है। क्षत्रियों को रक्षा के लिए ही शस्त्र उठाने चाहिए, चाहे वह व्यक्ति की हो या सम्पूर्ण समुदाय की। जो क्षत्रिय अपनी शक्ति का प्रदर्शन तदनुसार नहीं करता और अपनी जान गंवाने के डर से अपनी क्षमता के अनुसार कार्य नहीं करता, उसे चोर कहलाने के योग्य है।

महान बनने की इच्छा रखने वाले राजा को छह दोषों से बचना चाहिए: नींद, तंद्रा, भय, क्रोध, आलस्य और विलंब। इन छः गुणों को नहीं भूलना चाहिए: सत्य, दान, दया, परोपकार, क्षमा और धैर्य।

भारत - महानतम दर्शन और आध्यात्मिक संस्कृति का घर

प्राचीन भारत से आए सभी विज्ञान, गणित, वास्तुकला, कृषि और चिकित्सा विकास के अलावा, इसने दुनिया को महानतम दर्शन और आध्यात्मिक संस्कृति भी प्रदान की है जिसे कई देशों ने अपनाया है।

आत्मा, ईश्वर, पुनर्जन्म प्रणाली, कर्म, धर्म और योग प्रथाओं की शिक्षाएँ जो भारतीय प्रदान करते हैं, महान आध्यात्मिक अनुभवों के साथ आती हैं। इन शिक्षाओं को कभी भी बाहरी दुनिया पर लागू नहीं किया गया, बल्कि तर्क, समझ और संस्कृति के गहन ज्ञान ने उन्हें भारतीय वैदिक संस्कृति का अध्ययन कराया।

ब्रिटिश साम्राज्य के दौरान कुछ गलतफहमियों के कारण यह खजाना और ज्ञान इन दिनों गायब हो रहा है। भारत में वैदिक संस्कृति और दर्शन के बारे में लोगों को फिर से शिक्षित करके हम यह सच्चा और शुद्ध ज्ञान वापस पा सकते हैं।

कई समूहों ने पहले से ही प्राचीन वैदिक ग्रंथों के बारे में पढ़ाना शुरू कर दिया है। युवा पीढ़ी के लिए यह जानना जरूरी है।

हमारे पास अभी भी ऋग्वेद, अथर्ववेद, यजुर्वेद और सामवेद, ब्राह्मण, आरण्यक, उपनिषद, वेदांत सूत्र, रामायण और महाभारत जैसे इतिहास जिसमें भगवद गीता और पुराण शामिल हैं।

महान वैदिक संस्कृति का उल्लेख उस समय के कई महान लेखकों और साहित्यकारों ने किया है। लेखक फिलिप रॉसन ने दक्षिण पूर्व एशिया की कला में उल्लेख किया है: «भारत की संस्कृति दुनिया की सबसे शक्तिशाली सभ्यता शक्तियों में से एक रही है।»

चीन, कोरिया, तिब्बत और मंगोलिया जैसे सुदूर पूर्व के देश अपने लिए प्रेरणादायक विचार आयात करने के लिए भारत के ऋणी हैं।

हेनरी डेविड थोरौ ने कहा, «सुबह मैं अपनी बुद्धि को भगवद गीता के अद्त दर्शन से स्नान कराता हूँ।» दर्शनशास्त्र के इतिहास में डॉ. एनफील्ड कहते हैं, «हमने पाया कि पाइथागोरस ने ज्ञान प्राप्त करने के उद्देश्य से भारत का दौरा किया था, एनाक्सार्चस, पायरो और अन्य जो बाद में ग्रीस में महान दार्शनिक बन गए।»

नेहरू द्वारा लिखित «द डिस्कवरी ऑफ इंडिया» के ग्रंथों के अनुसार, ऐसा लगता है कि जैसे-जैसे लोग वैदिक आध्यात्मिक दर्शन के विभागों को फिर से खोजते हैं, वे इसे फिर बड़े चाव से स्वीकार करेंगे।

एनी बेसेंट ने भी भारत की संस्कृति की सराहना की थी; उन्होंने कहा कि महाभारत और गीता जैसे महाकाव्यों की कीमत कम है।

वह अपनी किताब में कहती हैं, «हिंदू भारत की जीवन रेखाएं हैं, लगभग 40 वर्षों के अध्ययन के बाद, मुझे कोई भी इतना परिपूर्ण, इतना दार्शनिक नहीं मिला जितना कि महान धर्म हिंदू धर्म। जितना अधिक आप इसे जानेंगे, उतना अधिक आप इसे पसंद करेंगे, जितना अधिक आप इसे समझेंगे, उतना अधिक आप इसे महत्व देंगे।»

सच तो यह है कि भारतीय अपनी भारतीय संस्कृति की उतनी कद्र नहीं करते जितनी उन्हें करनी चाहिए। समस्या यह है कि पिछली कई पीढ़ियों से वैदिक संस्कृति भारत से लुप्त होती जा रही है। भारतीयों को अपनी संस्कृति में कोई रुचि नहीं दिखती। लोग योग शिक्षक की तलाश में कैलिफोर्निया जाते हैं, लेकिन सच्चाई यह है कि कई विदेशी भारत आते हैं, सर्वश्रेष्ठ योग शिक्षक पाने के लिए पैसे बचाते हैं।

भारत ने कैसे खोई अपनी पहचान

बहुत से लोग सोचते हैं कि दुनिया में इतना बड़ा योगदान देने के बावजूद भारत ने अपनी पहचान क्यों खो दी। भारत के उपनिवेशीकरण के दौरान, अंग्रेजों द्वारा पारंपरिक प्रणालियों को हटाने के लिए व्यवस्थित तरीके से एक प्रवृत्ति स्थापित की गई थी। यह चलन आज़ादी के बाद भी जारी रहा।

इसके अलावा, विद्वानों का एक समूह किसी भी तरह से हिंदुओं को ईसाई धर्म में परिवर्तित करने में रुचि रखता था।

ऑक्सफोर्ड विश्वविद्यालय में संस्कृत के प्रोफेसर सर मोनियर विलियम्स के अनुसार, एक फाउंडेशन का उद्देश्य धर्मग्रंथों का संस्कृत में अनुवाद करना था ताकि वे भारत के स्थानीय लोगों से आसानी से संवाद कर सकें।

दूसरा एजेंडा अंग्रेजों द्वारा शुरू की गई शिक्षा प्रणाली थी।

टी.बी. मैकाले का उद्देश्य अधिकतम हिंदुओं को ईसाई धर्म में परिवर्तित करना था ताकि भारतीय लोग ब्रिटिश (अंग्रेजी) प्रशासन के साथ अधिक उचित सहयोग कर सकें।

इस उद्देश्य से, मैकाले ने 1836 में भारत में शिक्षा बोर्ड के अध्यक्ष के रूप में अपने पिता को लिखा:

"हमारे अंग्रेजी स्कूल अच्छी तरह फल-फूल रहे हैं। यदि हमारी शिक्षा की योजनाओं का पालन किया जाए तो बंगाल में सम्मानित वर्गों के बीच एक भी मूर्तिपूजक नहीं रहेगा; "मैं इस प्रोजेक्ट का दिल से आनंद लेता हूं। संस्कृत भाषा उतनी महत्वपूर्ण नहीं है जितनी अंग्रेजी।"

"हमें एक ऐसा वर्ग बनाने के लिए अपना सर्वश्रेष्ठ प्रयास करना चाहिए जो हमारे और उन लाखों लोगों के बीच संवाद कर सके जिन पर हम शासन करते हैं।"

एक ऐसा वर्ग, जो रक्त और रंग में भारतीय हो, लेकिन स्वाद, राय, नैतिकता और बुद्धि में अंग्रेजी।

मैकाले वर्तमान प्रशासन के पक्ष में नहीं थे क्योंकि वह सीमित साधनों के साथ अपना स्वयं का अंग्रेजी वर्ग विकसित करना चाहते थे, ताकि सभी लोगों को इस अंग्रेजी संस्कृति की आदत हो जाए।

मैकाले की योजना भारत की वैदिक संस्कृति को खत्म करना और भारत के लोगों को इसकी सभी प्रगति, विज्ञान और तकनीक को भुला देना था। विश्व प्रगति में योगदान; और ब्रिटिश व्यवस्था इस योजना में सफल हो गयी।

इसीलिए भारतीय पुनः अपनी स्थिति और उच्च विकास प्राप्त करने में असमर्थ रहे।

यह मत भूलिए कि जिन उपलब्धियों ने भारत का मान बढ़ाया है उनमें आज भी भारतीय शामिल हैं। आज भी भारत के छात्र दुनिया के सबसे प्रतिभाशाली छात्रों में से एक हैं।

लेखक ने अमेरिका में देखा है कि कक्षा में अधिकांश टॉपर्स भारत से होते हैं।

भारत पहले की तरह प्रगतिशील हो सकता है। भ्रष्टाचार व्यापक है और हम केवल इसका पालन करके ही इस पर काबू पा सकते हैं।

कृषि

पूरी दुनिया में कृषि का व्यापार 4 ट्रिलियन डॉलर है।

18वीं सदी तक भारत में 83% खेती होती थी। 19वीं सदी तक यह घटकर 70% रह गई। 1970 आते-आते यह 43% रह गई, और 2024 में यह केवल 15% रह गई है। 18वीं सदी तक हम पूरी दुनिया में 33% खाद्यान्न का निर्यात करते थे, जो आज केवल 0.3% रह गया है। 18वीं सदी में गरीबी नहीं थी।

अभी भारत में लगभग 50 करोड़ लोग बेरोजगार हैं।

18वीं सदी में हम जैविक बीज और जैविक खाद का प्रयोग करके पौष्टिक खेती का उत्पादन करते थे जिससे हमारे रासायनिक और उर्वरक के खर्च भी बचते थे और लोग स्वस्थ और खुशहाल रहते थे।

आज भारत में हर साल रासायनिक और उर्वरक का खर्चा 60,000 करोड़ रुपये है और 120 बिलियन रुपये दवाइयों का खर्चा है।

इंडोनेशिया ने खेती छोड़ दी और आज उस देश में एक डॉलर की कीमत 16,500 इंडोनेशियाई मुद्रा के बराबर है। अभी भारत में डॉलर की कीमत 80 रुपये है। अगर हमने भी खेती करना छोड़ दिया तो इंडोनेशिया बनने में ज्यादा समय नहीं लगेगा।

अगर खेती को नहीं बचाएंगे तो देश नहीं बचेगा। विश्व में मानव सभ्यता के कल्याण के लिए पूरे देश को जैविक खेती और जैविक खाद का प्रयोग करना ही पड़ेगा।

बिल और मेलिंडा गेट्स फाउंडेशन और रॉकफेलर फाउंडेशन ने जैविक बीजों का बैंक बनाया है जिसका नाम है सीड वॉल्ट। इसमें लगभग 45 लाख जैविक बीज, जो कि पूरे विश्व से लिए गए हैं, एकत्रित किए गए हैं।

आनुवंशिक रूप से संशोधित जीव (जीएमओ) का मतलब है, किसी जीव की विशेषताओं को बदलने के लिए, आमतौर पर उच्च तकनीक आनुवंशिक इंजीनियरिंग का उपयोग करके जीनोम में एक या अधिक परिवर्तन किए गए पौधा, जानवर या सूक्ष्म जीव। जीएमओ को जैव प्रौद्योगिकी के अधीन किया जाता है। जीएमओ को बनाने के लिए, किसी जीव के डीएनए से वांछित जीन को लक्षित रूप से हटाकर दूसरे जीव में जोड़ा जाता है।

जीएमओ और मोनसेंटो कंपनी की खाद्य बीज में पूरे विश्व में तानाशाही है। पहले इन्होंने हरित क्रांति के नाम से पूरी दुनिया में रासायनिक और उर्वरक बेचना शुरू किया। हरित क्रांति के नाम पर पूरे विश्व में कृषि उत्पादन में जबरदस्त नुकसान हुआ, जिसकी वजह से आज करोड़ों हेक्टेयर जमीन बंजर हो गई और किसानों को बेरोजगार बनाकर आत्महत्या करने पर मजबूर किया गया।

जीएमओ कंपनी पूरी दुनिया के 39 देशों में प्रतिबंधित है लेकिन भारत में अभी भी 90% कृषि बाजार में जीएमओ का राज है। उदाहरण के लिए, गेहूं, चावल, कपास आदि के हाइब्रिड बीज जीएमओ कंपनियां बेचती हैं।

मृदा स्वास्थ्य और किसानों के कल्याण के लिए व्यावहारिक समाधान

1. वर्तमान कानूनों का पालन: कृषि संस्थानों द्वारा कृषि इनपुट पर कोई भी सिफारिश वर्तमान खाद्य कानूनों का पालन करना चाहिए।

2. मिट्टी की उर्वरता को राष्ट्रीय संपत्ति घोषित करना: मिट्टी की उर्वरता को राष्ट्रीय संपत्ति या राष्ट्रीय धरोहर घोषित किया जाए। इसे हर कीमत पर बनाए रखना कृषि विभागों की जिम्मेदारी होनी चाहिए। रासायनिक उद्योगों के उत्पादन में वृद्धि के दावों के बावजूद दुनिया भर में मिट्टी की उर्वरता कम हो गई है।

3. सिंचाई को नमीकरण में बदलना: मिट्टी, फसलों, फसलों के पोषक मूल्य को बचाने के साथ-साथ ऊर्जा और पानी के संरक्षण के लिए ‹सिंचाई› शब्द को ‹नमीकरण› में बदल दिया जाना चाहिए।

4. उपज की परिभाषा: ‹उपज› शब्द को परिभाषित करने की आवश्यकता है। क्या यह केवल सकल वजन है? या फिर इसका संबंध उसके खाद्य मूल्य के साथ-साथ खाद्य कानूनों के अनुपालन और भोजन की गुणवत्ता से भी होना चाहिए?

5. उर्वरक की परिभाषा: ‹उर्वरक› शब्द को स्पष्ट रूप से परिभाषित करने की आवश्यकता है। बूस्टर और प्रामाणिक उर्वरकों के बीच अंतर को स्पष्ट रूप से बताया जाना चाहिए।

6. वैदिक कृषि की शिक्षा: हमें वृक्षायुर्वेद, अग्निहोत्र, पंचांग, प्रकाश निघंटु आदि सभी प्राचीन विषयों को शामिल करते हुए वैदिक कृषि पढ़ाना शुरू करना होगा।

7. सब्सिडी देना बंद करें: सब्सिडी देना बंद करें, आप किसान का गौरव छीन रहे हैं और उसे भिखारी बना रहे हैं। खेती व्यवसाय का सम्मान बहाल करें। सब्सिडी देने के बजाय, किसानों को उचित मूल्य दें, यानी लागत मूल्य और मुनाफा। किसान का शोषण बंद करें। आइए हम अपनी संस्कृति की ओर लौटें और इसे दुनिया भर में प्रचारित करें। वर्तमान व्यवस्था के साथ हम कभी भी स्थिरता तक नहीं पहुंच सकते।

स्थिरता प्राप्त करने के लिए हमारी संपूर्ण सामाजिक-आर्थिक संरचना को वैदिक तरीकों में बदलने की जरूरत है, खासकर खेती में!

भारतीय चिकित्सा

पूरी दुनिया जानती है कि जब कोरोना जैसी महामारी आई तो लोग बचने के लिए पारंपरिक चिकित्सा पद्धति की ओर लौटे। भारत के आयुर्वेदिक ज्ञान ने भारत सहित पूरी दुनिया की रक्षा की और आयुर्वेद की शक्ति का ज्ञान पूरी दुनिया को हुआ।

पूरी दुनिया में दवाइयों का व्यापार ₹500 लाख करोड़ है।

जब से हमने आयुर्वेद को छोड़कर आधुनिक चिकित्सा की ओर रुख किया है, तब से अब तक भारत दुनिया का सबसे अधिक बीमार देश बन गया है। यदि हम आयुर्वेद पर काम करते हैं, तो यह भारत के लिए सबसे बड़ा अवसर है। भारत अपने कुल जीडीपी का 2.6% चिकित्सा और स्वास्थ्य पर खर्च करता है, जबकि बाकी देश 8 से 9% खर्च करते हैं।

भारत पूरी दुनिया में दवाइयों का निर्यात सिर्फ 2.6% करता है, जो लगभग $22 बिलियन है। भारत 80% दवाइयों का कच्चा माल चीन से खरीदता है, जो एक बहुत गंभीर समस्या है जिसे बहुत जल्दी हल करना होगा। इस समस्या से बचने के लिए हमें जैविक

अन्न खाना बहुत जरूरी है, क्योंकि बड़े-बड़े डॉक्टर कहते हैं कि हम जैसा खाते हैं, हमारा शरीर वैसा बन जाता है।

यहां पर विषय यह है कि खेती और दवाइयों का क्या संबंध है। अब हम पारंपरिक भारतीय चिकित्सा में प्रयोग होने वाली आयुर्वेदिक जड़ी-बूटियों तथा खेती का विस्तार से वर्णन करते हैं।

पूरे विश्व में जड़ी-बूटियों का व्यापार $216 बिलियन का है, और एक अनुमान के मुताबिक 2032 तक यह बढ़कर $440 बिलियन तक पहुंच जाएगा। WHO के अनुसार, जड़ी-बूटियों का व्यापार प्रतिवर्ष 15% बढ़ रहा है। पूरे विश्व में कोरोना के बाद जड़ी-बूटियों की लोकप्रियता बहुत अधिक बढ़ी है, जिससे उनके व्यापार में भारी वृद्धि हो रही है। जड़ी-बूटियों की मांग बहुत अधिक है, लेकिन इसका उत्पादन बहुत कम है। चीन के बाद, भारत विश्व का दूसरा सबसे बड़ा जड़ी-बूटियों का निर्यातक देश है। चीन और भारत मिलकर पूरे विश्व की 70% जड़ी-बूटियों की मांग पूरी करते हैं। भारत की जैव विविधता इस प्रकार है कि यहां विश्व में सबसे अधिक और सबसे अच्छी गुणवत्ता की जड़ी-बूटियों का उत्पादन किया जाता है। पूरी दुनिया में 16 जलवायु क्षेत्र हैं, और भारत ही एकमात्र ऐसा देश है जहां सभी 16 जलवायु पाई जाती हैं। जैसे, मेघालय में वर्षा वन, राजस्थान में रेगिस्तान, उत्तर भारत में हिमालयी क्षेत्र आदि। सभी जलवायु होने की वजह से भारत में विभिन्न प्रकार के फल, सब्जियां, मसाले, दालें और जड़ी-बूटियाँ बहुत अच्छी गुणवत्ता और मात्रा में उत्पादन की जाती हैं।

हिमालय में मौजूद अकेले गंधमर्दन पर्वत में 16,000 से अधिक दुर्लभ जड़ी-बूटियाँ पाई जाती हैं।

बांस के व्यापार का भविष्य

विश्व में बांस का व्यापार $65 बिलियन प्रतिवर्ष है और यह 2030 तक $94 बिलियन तक पहुंच जाएगा।

बांस में निवेश और निवेश पर प्रतिफल (ROI):

- निवेश का उदाहरण: यदि आप 10 एकड़ बांस की खेती में ₹15 लाख निवेश करते हैं, तो 5 वर्ष बाद आपको 70 वर्ष तक हर वर्ष ₹15 लाख मिलेंगे।
- ROI: अर्थात् ₹15 लाख निवेश पर ₹10.5 करोड़ प्रतिफल।

प्रमुख बांस परियोजनाएं:

- लंदन में 80 मंजिलों वाला पहला बांस टावर।
- टोक्यो में दुनिया का सबसे ऊंचा बांस टावर बनाने का काम शुरू।

बांस से बने उत्पाद:

- लकड़ी उद्योग
- वानिकी
- लुगदी और कागज उद्योग
- वस्त्र उद्योग
- जैव ऊर्जा उद्योग
- खाद्य और पेय पदार्थ उद्योग
- ऑटोमोटिव उद्योग
- और भी बहुत कुछ

भारत हर साल ₹2,400 करोड़ का बांस आयात करता है। चीन बांस का सबसे बड़ा निर्यातक है।

अतः उद्योगपति और किसान मिलकर बांस में निवेश कर बहुत अधिक मुनाफा कमा सकते हैं जिससे भारतीय अर्थव्यवस्था को मजबूत किया जा सकता है।

चंदन व्यवसाय का भविष्य

चंदन व्यवसाय का मूल्य प्रतिवर्ष $300 मिलियन है।

अंतर्राष्ट्रीय मांग:

- चंदन की अंतर्राष्ट्रीय मांग प्रति वर्ष लगभग 10,000 मीट्रिक टन होने का अनुमान है।
- बड़ी मांग और कम आपूर्ति:
    - भारतीय चंदन की वार्षिक वैश्विक मांग 28,000 टन है।
    - कानूनी चंदन की भारतीय वार्षिक आपूर्ति केवल 200 टन है।
    - पिछले 10 वर्षों में चंदन की आधिकारिक आपूर्ति में 90% की गिरावट आई है।
    - चंदन की प्राकृतिक जनसंख्या लगभग समाप्त हो चुकी है।

लोकप्रियता:

- भारतीय चंदन विश्व में सबसे लोकप्रिय है।

- ऑस्ट्रेलिया भारतीय चंदन का सबसे बड़ा उत्पादक है।
- ऑस्ट्रेलियाई कंपनी गैलडर्मा कंपनी को चंदन तेल $5000 प्रति किलोग्राम बेचती है।

चंदन से बने उत्पाद:

- उत्तम फर्नीचर और हस्तशिल्प
- भारतीय चंदन कोर लॉग
- धार्मिक अनुष्ठान और समारोह
- दवाइयाँ
- इत्र
- सौंदर्य प्रसाधन
- प्राकृतिक दवा
- अरोमाथेरेपी

चंदन की खेती:

निवेश और प्रतिफल:

- निवेश: ₹15 लाख
- रिटर्न: 10 साल में ₹2.5 करोड़

1 एकड़ में पौधे और लागत:

- बड़ी मांग और कम आपूर्ति
- सफेद चंदन: 375 पौधे
- कौरिना: 125 पौधे
- देसी नीम: 125 पौधे
- लाल चंदन: 125 पौधे
- मीठी नीम: 750 पौधे
- ड्रिप सिंचाई
- सौर विद्त बाड़ लगाना
- वार्षिक निराई और मिट्टी की जुताई
- देसी खाद
- सुरक्षा और श्रम शुल्क

अनुमानित निवेश:

- 10 साल के लिए अनुमानित निवेश ₹12 से ₹18 लाख होगा, जो शहर, मिट्टी के स्वास्थ्य आदि पर निर्भर करता है।
- यदि जमीन चाहिए तो हम आपकी आवश्यकतानुसार सहयोग कर सकते हैं या किराए पर व्यवस्था कर सकते हैं।

भांग के व्यापार का भविष्य

वैश्विक भांग बाजार का आकार 2021 में $5.7 बिलियन था और पूर्वानुमानित अवधि (2023-2030) के दौरान 14.04% की सीएजीआर पर 2022 में $6.54 बिलियन से बढ़कर 2030 तक $18.71 बिलियन होने की उम्मीद है।

लाइसेंस और कानूनी स्थिति:

- राष्ट्रीय कानून के तहत मेडिकल कैनबिस की अनुमति है, और ड्रग्स और कॉस्मेटिक्स अधिनियम के तहत निर्मित सीबीडी तेल को कानूनी रूप से प्राप्त और उपयोग किया जा सकता है।

- औषधि एवं प्रसाधन सामग्री अधिनियम के अनुसार, कानूनी भांग में 0.3 प्रतिशत से अधिक THC नहीं होना चाहिए।

बड़ी मांग-कम आपूर्ति:

- भांग को मारिजुआना और सीबीडी के नाम से भी जाना जाता है।
- कनाडा भांग के तेल का सबसे बड़ा निर्यातक है।

कनाडा ने **2022** में न्यूजीलैंड और दक्षिण कोरिया सहित कई व्यापार भागीदारों को 514 मीट्रिक टन गांजा तेल का निर्यात किया, जिसका कुल मूल्य $4.5 मिलियन से अधिक था। संयुक्त राज्य अमेरिका को होने वाले गांजे के तेल के निर्यात की कुल मात्रा 403 मीट्रिक टन और मूल्य $3.8 मिलियन था।

- चीन ने पिछले 5 वर्षों में भांग में भारी निवेश और अनुसंधान किया है।
- दुनिया भर में कुल 606 पेटेंट हैं, जिनमें से 309 चीन के पास हैं।
- इस वर्ष थाईलैंड और मलेशिया ने भांग को वैध किया।
- विश्व स्तर पर 34 देशों ने भांग को दवा और औषधीय उपयोग की अनुमति दी है।
- पौधे के मामले में चीन एक महाशक्ति बन गया है।
- जर्मनी इस वर्ष दुनिया का सबसे बड़ा चिकित्सा भांग बाजार बन गया है।
- अमेरिका और अन्य बड़े देशों ने इसे वैध बनाया है और भारी निवेश किया है।

आर्थिक संभावनाएं:

- भांग प्रति हेक्टेयर ₹105,000 ($1,500) से अधिक की आय लाता है।
- लेवी की पहली जींस और जैकेट 69% कपास और 31% भांग से बनी थीं।

भारत में स्थिति:

- भारत में भांग का कुछ हिस्सा वैध है।
- यदि हम अधिक जानकारी जुटाएं, अनुसंधान और विकास करें, और ₹1 लाख करोड़ का निवेश करें, तो यह अगले कुछ वर्षों में भारत के लिए एक महत्वपूर्ण व्यवसाय बन सकता है।
- भारतीय हिमालय, विशेषकर उत्तराखंड, भांग की खेती के लिए सबसे अच्छी भूमि प्रदान करता है।

विश्व कपड़ा व्यापार

बाजार मूल्यांकन:

- 2023 में, वैश्विक कपड़ा बाजार का मूल्य $1,837.27 बिलियन था।
- 2024 से 2030 तक, यह राजस्व में 7.4% की चक्रवृद्धि वार्षिक वृद्धि दर (CAGR) से बढ़ने का अनुमान है।

ऐतिहासिक संदर्भ:

- 1800वीं सदी से पहले, भारत का कपड़ा क्षेत्र में एकाधिकार था।
- भारत का कपड़ा और परिधान उद्योग देश की जीडीपी में लगभग 2.3%, औद्योगिक उत्पादन में 13% और निर्यात में 12% योगदान देता है।
- कपड़ा उद्योग लगभग 45 मिलियन लोगों को प्रत्यक्ष और अप्रत्यक्ष रूप से रोजगार देता है, जिससे यह कृषि के बाद भारत में रोजगार का दूसरा सबसे बड़ा प्रदाता बन जाता है।

प्रमुख तथ्य:

- जूट: भारत विश्व का सबसे बड़ा जूट उत्पादक है, जो विश्व के उत्पादन का लगभग 62.2% और कुल क्षेत्रफल का 59.3% है। 2022 वित्तीय वर्ष में, भारत ने लगभग 660 हजार हेक्टेयर कटाई क्षेत्र से एक मिलियन मीट्रिक टन से अधिक जूट का उत्पादन किया। भारत जूट के सामान का दुनिया का दूसरा सबसे बड़ा निर्यातक भी है।
- रेशम: भारत दुनिया का दूसरा सबसे बड़ा रेशम उत्पादक है।
- कपास: भारत दुनिया का सबसे बड़ा कपास उत्पादक है। 2022-2023 में, भारत ने 5.84 मिलियन मीट्रिक टन कपास का उत्पादन किया, जो दुनिया के कुल कपास उत्पादन का 23.83% है। भारत दुनिया में फाइबर का दूसरा सबसे बड़ा उत्पादक भी है।

आर्थिक तुलना:

- फ्रांसीसी कंपनी क्रिश्चियन डायर का कारोबार €86.2 बिलियन है, जो भारत के कुल कपड़ा निर्यात से भी अधिक है।
- भारत का कपड़ा निर्यात केवल $45 बिलियन है।

उभरते रुझान:

- दुनिया में कई कंपनियाँ भांग, बांस, और जैविक कपास का उत्पादन शुरू कर रही हैं।
- फैशन उद्योग तेल के बाद दूसरा सबसे अधिक प्रदूषण फैलाने वाला उद्योग है।

मोनसेंटो के बीटी कपास के बीज:

- भारत का 90% और चीन का 80% बीटी कपास का उपयोग कर रहा है।
- भारत दुनिया का दूसरा सबसे बड़ा कपास उत्पादक है, चीन के बाद।
- मोनसेंटो के बीटी कपास के बीज बड़े पैमाने पर विफल होने के बाद भारत में 3,00,000 से अधिक किसानों ने आत्महत्या की है।
- हर साल दुनिया भर में लगभग 1 मिलियन लोगों के आत्महत्या करने की सूचना है।

मुद्दे और समाधान:

- बीज पर पेटेंट के माध्यम से, मोनसेंटो हमारे ग्रह का «जीवन भगवान» बन गया है, जो किसानों और मूल प्रजनकों से जीवन के नवीनीकरण के लिए किराया वसूलता है।
- यदि भारत जैविक कपड़ा कृषि, जैविक बीज, भांग कपड़ा, बांस कपड़ा शुरू करता है, तो हम किसानों को बचा सकते हैं, भारत को बचा सकते हैं और दुनिया को बचा सकते हैं।

विश्व निर्माण व्यवसाय

बाजार मूल्यांकन:

- वैश्विक निर्माण व्यवसाय का वर्तमान और स्वीकृत मूल्य $15.97 ट्रिलियन है।

प्रौद्योगिकी: सीमेंट बनाम चूना पत्थर (चूना):

- सीमेंट: अधिकतम जीवनकाल 100 वर्ष।
- चूना पत्थर: न्यूनतम जीवनकाल 500 वर्ष।

उत्पादन क्षमता:

- 2024 तक, सीमेंट उत्पादन क्षमता 1 बिलियन टन प्रति वर्ष होने का अनुमान है।
- भारत दुनिया का दूसरा सबसे बड़ा सीमेंट उत्पादक है।

पर्यावरणीय प्रभाव:

- सामान्य सीमेंट आमतौर पर 7 दिनों में 89-90 कैलोरी/ग्राम और 28 दिनों में 90-100 कैलोरी/ग्राम का उत्पादन करता है।
- सीमेंट निर्माण सामग्री वैश्विक कार्बन डाइऑक्साइड उत्सर्जन का 9% हिस्सा है, जो दुनिया के सभी ट्रकों से निकलने वाली कार्बन डाइऑक्साइड से भी अधिक है।

स्थायित्व चिंताएँ:

- मुंबई के पास वाशी ब्रिज और गोवा में मंडोवी नदी पुल जैसे कई पुल, ओवरहेड टैंक, बहुमंजिला कंक्रीट आवासीय इमारतें आदि टिकाऊ नहीं हैं।
- भारतीय चूना पत्थर प्रौद्योगिकी दुनिया में सबसे पुरानी है।

चूना पत्थर प्रौद्योगिकी के लाभ:

- चूना पत्थर प्रौद्योगिकी से निर्मित भारत के मंदिर 5000 साल से अधिक पुराने हैं। राम सेतु पुल लगभग 10000 साल पुराना है।
- चूना लेपित इमारतें अंदर 9% तक ठंडा तापमान अनुभव कर सकती हैं।

आर्थिक प्रभाव:

- यदि हम सीमेंट का इस्तेमाल जारी रखते हैं, तो हर 100 साल में पूरे भारत का पैसा सिर्फ पुनर्निर्माण में चला जाएगा।

सिफारिशें:

- चूना पत्थर, बांस, हेमपक्रेट, और सेल्फ हीलिंग कंक्रीट का उपयोग शुरू करें ताकि भारत और दुनिया को बचाया जा सके।
- अंग्रेजों ने भारत से चूना पत्थर की तकनीक को खत्म कर दिया।
- अंग्रेजों ने हमेशा भारत में ढाका मुलमुल, हथकरघा बुनाई, आयुर्वेद और गुरुकुल प्रणाली जैसी किसी भी स्वदेशी सामग्री या प्रणाली के उपयोग को हतोत्साहित किया और इसके बजाय अपने आयातित संस्करणों की पेशकश की, विशेष रूप से पुरानी भारत की स्वदेशी प्रणालियों को खत्म करने के लिए।
- उनके शासन के दौरान निर्माण में चूने का उपयोग भी ऐसा ही हुआ।

अगर हम सीमेंट का उपयोग जारी रखते हैं, तो हर 100 साल में पूरे भारत का पैसा सिर्फ पुनर्निर्माण में चला जाएगा।

चूना पत्थर, बांस, हेमपक्रेट, और सेल्फ हीलिंग कंक्रीट का उपयोग शुरू करें, ताकि भारत और दुनिया को बचाया जा सके।

वैश्विक लॉजिस्टिक्स बाजार का आकार

2022 में वैश्विक लॉजिस्टिक्स बाजार का आकार 7.98 ट्रिलियन अमेरिकी डॉलर था और 2023 से 2030 तक 10.7% की उल्लेखनीय सीएजीआर के साथ 2030 तक इसका मूल्य लगभग 18.23 ट्रिलियन अमेरिकी डॉलर होने की उम्मीद है।

प्रमुख जानकारी:

- मार्केटलाइन की रिपोर्ट के अनुसार, सड़क माल ढुलाई और रसद वैश्विक परिवहन सेवा बाज़ार में अग्रणी खंड का प्रतिनिधित्व करते हैं, जो मूल्य के मामले में समग्र उद्योग के 74% से अधिक के लिए ज़िम्मेदार है।
- वैश्विक माल ढुलाई क्षेत्र 12.4 ट्रिलियन FTKS (फ्रेट टन-किलोमीटर) से अधिक की मात्रा तक पहुँच जाएगा।
- मूल्य के मामले में दुनिया के सड़क माल ढुलाई क्षेत्र में अमेरिका का हिस्सा 56% है।

ग्लोबल वार्मिंग पर प्रभाव:

- माल ढुलाई क्षेत्र अपने व्यापक रूप से जीवाश्म ईंधनों के उपयोग और परिणामी कार्बन उत्सर्जन के कारण ग्लोबल वार्मिंग में महत्वपूर्ण योगदान देता है।

सिफारिशें:

- वैश्विक सोचें, स्थानीय रहें - स्थानीय खरीदें:
- स्थानीय व्यवसायों का समर्थन करने और स्थानीय उपलब्ध उत्पादों को खरीदने से स्थानीय अर्थव्यवस्था को बढ़ावा मिलेगा।
- ऑनलाइन खरीदारी से बचें जब स्थानीय स्तर पर उत्पाद उपलब्ध हो, इससे परिवहन उत्सर्जन कम होता है और स्थानीय रोजगार का समर्थन होता है।
- भारत के स्थायी विकास के लिए एक मजबूत स्थानीय अर्थव्यवस्था आवश्यक है।

प्लास्टिक से पेट्रोल/बायोडीजल तक

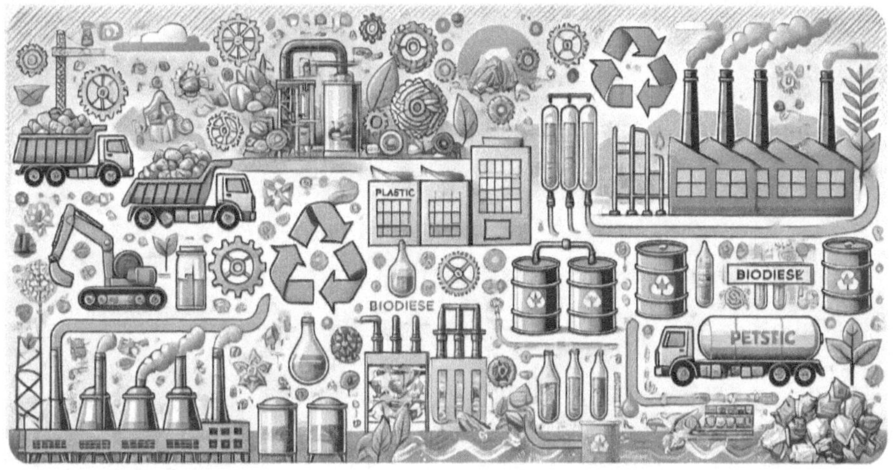

प्रमुख तथ्य:

- 1950 से 2019 तक 830 मिलियन टन प्लास्टिक कचरा उत्पन्न हुआ।
- केवल 10% प्लास्टिक को रीसाइकिल किया जाता है, जबकि 90% प्लास्टिक फेंक दिया जाता है।
- प्रतिदिन लाखों टन प्लास्टिक का उपयोग होता है।

अवसर:

- अंतिम ग्रेड प्लास्टिक से पेट्रोल/बायोडीजल और अन्य ईंधन बनाना।
- व्यवसाय शुरू करने की परियोजना लागत ₹10 लाख से ₹10 करोड़ तक होती है।

पॉलीहाइड्रॉक्सीब्यूटाइरेट (PHB)

विवरण:

- पीएचबी एक बायोडिग्रेडेबल पॉलिमर है जिसे बैक्टीरिया और आर्किया ऊर्जा और कार्बन रिजर्व के रूप में उत्पन्न करते हैं।
- यह माइक्रोबियल पॉलिस्टर के पॉलीहाइड्रॉक्सीअल्केनोएट्स (PHAs) परिवार का सदस्य है। पीएचबी का निर्माण सूक्ष्मजीवों की कोशिकाओं में होता है, जैसे कि ग्राम-पॉजिटिव और ग्राम-नेगेटिव बैक्टीरिया, जब वे पोषक तत्वों के तनाव या प्रतिकूल वातावरण का अनुभव करते हैं।

विशेषताएं:

- पीएचबी एक कठोर और भंगुर बहुलक है जिसमें थर्मोप्लास्टिक, हाइड्रोफोबिक और उच्च क्रिस्टलीय गुण होते हैं।
- यह एसिटाइल-सीओए से β-कीटोथियोलेज़, एसिटोएसिटाइल-सीओए रिडक्टेज़ और पीएचबी सिंथेज़ द्वारा उत्प्रेरित तीन एंजाइमेटिक प्रतिक्रियाओं के अनुक्रम द्वारा निर्मित होता है।

उत्पादन:

- पीएचबी मुख्य रूप से ग्लूकोज या स्टार्च से कार्बन आत्मसात का एक उत्पाद है, और सूक्ष्मजीव इसे ऊर्जा भंडारण अणु के रूप में उपयोग करते हैं जब अन्य सामान्य ऊर्जा स्रोत उपलब्ध नहीं होते हैं।

अनुप्रयोग:

- पीएचबी में पॉलीप्रोपाइलीन जैसे विभिन्न सिंथेटिक थर्मोप्लास्टिक्स के समान गुण हैं, जो इसे व्यापक अनुप्रयोगों और बायोडिग्रेडेबल प्लास्टिक के भविष्य के वाणिज्यिक बड़े पैमाने पर उत्पादन के लिए उपयोगी बनाता है।

हम एआई के युग में कृषि की बात क्यों कर रहे हैं?

आप सोच रहे होंगे कि हम एआई के युग में कृषि के बारे में क्यों बात कर रहे हैं। जब भारत की बात आती है, तो हमारे पूर्वज लाभ और नुकसान का सावधानीपूर्वक मूल्यांकन करने के बाद ही कोई निर्णय लेते थे। भारत की उत्कृष्ट शिक्षा प्रणाली ने हमें यह सिखाया कि दीर्घकालिक लाभ के लिए अल्पकालिक लाभ का त्याग न करें। हम थोड़े से नुकसान को सहन कर लेते थे, लेकिन हम अपनी आने वाली पीढ़ियों के लिए एक उज्ज्वल भविष्य की योजना बनाते थे।

आज लोग कृषि को एक साधारण व्यवसाय समझ रहे हैं और एआई में अरबों का निवेश कर रहे हैं। हालांकि, जल्दी पैसे कमाने की दौड़ में हम मानवता की बुनियादी जरूरतों को पूरा नहीं कर सकते हैं।

हरित क्रांति से सीख:

कृषि को उन्नत करने की हमारी जल्दबाजी में, हमने 1960 के दशक की हरित क्रांति के बाद अंधाधुंध रासायनिक और उर्वरकों का उपयोग किया। पिछले 65 वर्षों में, हमने 70% कृषि योग्य भूमि को नष्ट कर दिया है, और 10 में से 7 लोग बीमार हो गए हैं। आज, दुनिया महंगे कृषि उत्पादों को जैविक खेती के नाम पर बेच रही है, जिन्हें हम पारंपरिक कृषि के माध्यम से बहुत कम लागत में उत्पादन करते थे।

एक वैज्ञानिक रिपोर्ट से पता चला है कि मोबाइल विकिरण के कारण अगले 50 वर्षों में 10 में से 9 बच्चे शारीरिक और मानसिक रूप से विकलांग हो जाएंगे। जिस प्रकार रासायनिक उपयोग ने कृषि को विकलांग कर दिया है, अब हमारे पास एक स्थायी भविष्य की नींव रखने का अवसर है।

कृत्रिम बुद्धिमत्ता के नुकसान

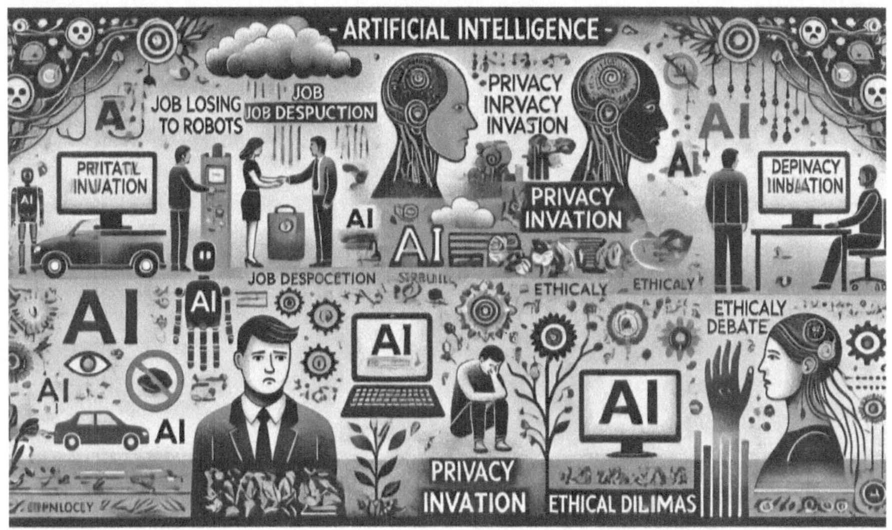

उच्च लागत:

ऐसी मशीनें बनाना जो मानव बुद्धि का अनुकरण कर सकें, एक महत्वपूर्ण उपलब्धि है जिसके लिए बहुत समय, संसाधनों और धन की आवश्यकता होती है। एआई को अद्यतित रहने और वर्तमान आवश्यकताओं को पूरा करने के लिए नवीनतम हार्डवेयर और सॉफ़्टवेयर की आवश्यकता होती है, जिससे यह काफी महंगा हो जाता है।

रचनात्मकता की कमी:

एआई लीक से हटकर नहीं सोच सकता। यह समय के साथ पूर्व-फेड डेटा और पिछले अनुभवों के साथ सीख सकता है, लेकिन अपने दृष्टिकोण में रचनात्मक नहीं हो सकता। उदाहरण के लिए, क्लिल जैसे बॉट फोर्ब्स के लिए केवल पूर्व-उपलब्ध डेटा और तथ्यों के आधार पर कमाई रिपोर्ट लिख सकते हैं। जबकि यह प्रभावशाली है कि एक बॉट स्वयं एक लेख लिख सकता है, लेकिन इसमें अन्य फोर्ब्स लेखों में मौजूद मानवीय स्पर्श का अभाव है।

बेरोजगारी:

एआई का एक अनुप्रयोग रोबोट है, जो कुछ मामलों में नौकरियों को विस्थापित कर रहा है और बेरोजगारी बढ़ा रहा है। उदाहरण के लिए, जापान जैसे कुछ तकनीकी रूप से उन्नत देशों में विनिर्माण व्यवसायों में मानव संसाधनों को प्रतिस्थापित करने के लिए अक्सर रोबोट का उपयोग किया जाता है। हालाँकि, यह हमेशा मामला नहीं होता है, क्योंकि यह मनुष्यों के लिए काम करने के अतिरिक्त अवसर पैदा करता है और साथ ही दक्षता बढ़ाने के लिए मनुष्यों की जगह लेता है।

मनुष्य को आलसी बनाना:

एआई एप्लिकेशन अधिकांश थकाऊ और दोहराव वाले कार्यों को स्वचालित करते हैं। चूँकि हमें काम पूरा करने के लिए चीजों को याद नहीं करना पड़ता या पहेलियाँ हल नहीं करनी पड़तीं, इसलिए हम अपने दिमाग का कम से कम उपयोग करते हैं। एआई की यह लत आने वाली पीढ़ियों के लिए समस्या पैदा कर सकती है।

कोई नैतिकता नहीं:

नैतिकता और नैतिकता महत्वपूर्ण मानवीय विशेषताएँ हैं जिन्हें एआई में शामिल करना मुश्किल हो सकता है। एआई की तीव्र प्रगति ने कई चिंताएँ पैदा कर दी हैं कि एक दिन, एआई अनियंत्रित रूप से बढ़ेगा, और अंततः मानवता को मिटा देगा। इस क्षण को एआई विलक्षणता के रूप में जाना जाता है।

भावनाशून्य:

बचपन से ही हमें सिखाया गया है कि न तो कंप्यूटर और न ही अन्य मशीनों में भावनाएँ होती हैं। मनुष्य एक टीम के रूप में कार्य करता है, और लक्ष्यों को प्राप्त करने के लिए टीम प्रबंधन आवश्यक है। हालाँकि, इस बात से इनकार नहीं किया जा सकता है कि प्रभावी ढंग से काम करने के मामले में रोबोट इंसानों से बेहतर हैं, लेकिन यह भी सच है कि मानवीय कनेक्शन, जो टीमों का आधार बनते हैं, उन्हें कंप्यूटर द्वारा प्रतिस्थापित नहीं किया जा सकता है।

कोई सुधार नहीं:

मनुष्य कृत्रिम बुद्धिमत्ता को पूर्व-लोड किए गए तथ्यों और अनुभव पर आधारित तकनीक से अधिक विकसित नहीं कर सकता। एआई एक ही कार्य को बार-बार करने में कुशल है, लेकिन यदि हम कोई समायोजन या सुधार चाहते हैं, तो हमें कोड को मैन्युअल रूप से

बदलना होगा। एआई को मानव बुद्धि की तरह एक्सेस और उपयोग नहीं किया जा सकता है, लेकिन यह अनंत डेटा संग्रहीत कर सकता है। मशीनें केवल वही कार्य पूरा कर सकती हैं जिनके लिए उन्हें विकसित या प्रोग्राम किया गया है; यदि उनसे कुछ और पूरा करने के लिए कहा जाता है, तो वे अक्सर असफल हो जाते हैं या बेकार परिणाम देते हैं, जिसके महत्वपूर्ण नकारात्मक प्रभाव हो सकते हैं।

स्वास्थ्य देखभाल में ए.आई

स्वास्थ्य देखभाल में एआई का नुकसान नैतिक और गोपनीयता संबंधी चिंताओं की संभावना है। स्वास्थ्य देखभाल में एआई सिस्टम संवेदनशील चिकित्सा जानकारी सहित रोगी डेटा पर बहुत अधिक निर्भर करते हैं। यह सुनिश्चित करने की आवश्यकता है कि यह डेटा सुरक्षित और गोपनीयता-सचेत तरीके से एकत्र, संग्रहीत और उपयोग किया जाए। रोगी की गोपनीयता की रक्षा करना, डेटा गोपनीयता बनाए रखना और व्यक्तिगत स्वास्थ्य जानकारी तक अनधिकृत पहुंच को रोकना महत्वपूर्ण विचार हैं।

मार्केटिंग में एआई

मार्केटिंग में एआई का एक नुकसान मानवीय स्पर्श और रचनात्मकता की संभावित कमी है। जबकि एआई विभिन्न विपणन कार्यों को स्वचालित कर सकता है और डेटा-संचालित अंतर्दृष्टि उत्पन्न कर सकता है, यह विपणन के अद्वितीय मानवीय तत्वों, जैसे भावनात्मक संबंध, अंतर्ज्ञान और रचनात्मक सोच को दोहराने के लिए संघर्ष कर सकता है। एआई एल्गोरिदम पूरी तरह से डेटा और पूर्वनिर्धारित पैटर्न पर निर्भर हो सकते हैं, संभावित रूप से उन नवीन या आउट-ऑफ-द-बॉक्स मार्केटिंग दृष्टिकोणों से चूक जाते हैं जिनके लिए मानव रचनात्मकता और अंतर्ज्ञान की आवश्यकता होती है।

शिक्षा में ए.आई

शिक्षा में एआई का एक नुकसान नैतिक और गोपनीयता संबंधी चिंताओं की संभावना है। एआई सिस्टम छात्रों के प्रदर्शन, व्यवहार और व्यक्तिगत जानकारी सहित महत्वपूर्ण मात्रा में डेटा एकत्र और विश्लेषण करता है। यह सुनिश्चित करने की आवश्यकता है कि इस डेटा को उचित गोपनीयता सुरक्षा उपायों के साथ सुरक्षित रूप से संभाला जाए।

रचनात्मकता में एआई

रचनात्मकता में एआई का एक नुकसान एआई-जनित रचनात्मक कार्यों में मौलिकता और प्रामाणिकता की संभावित कमी है। जबकि एआई सिस्टम मौजूदा शैलियों और पैटर्न की

नकल कर सकते हैं, इस बारे में बहस चल रही है कि क्या एआई वास्तव में मनुष्यों के समान रचनात्मकता रख सकता है। एआई-जनित कार्यों में मानवीय अनुभवों और भावनाओं से आने वाली गहराई, भावनात्मक जुड़ाव और अद्वितीय दृष्टिकोण की कमी हो सकती है।

परिवहन में ए.आई

परिवहन में एआई का नुकसान इसके द्वारा प्रस्तुत नैतिक और कानूनी चुनौतियाँ हैं। उदाहरण के लिए, स्वायत्त वाहन दुर्घटनाओं की स्थिति में दायित्व के बारे में सवाल उठाते हैं। यह निर्धारित करना कि एआई-नियंत्रित वाहन के टकराव में शामिल होने पर कौन जिम्मेदार है, जटिल हो सकता है। इसके अतिरिक्त, एआई सिस्टम द्वारा लिए गए निर्णय, जैसे कि यातायात प्रबंधन या दुर्घटना से बचाव से संबंधित निर्णय, नैतिक विचारों पर विचार करने की आवश्यकता हो सकती है, जैसे सीमित संसाधनों का आवंटन या यात्रियों बनाम पैदल यात्रियों की सुरक्षा। इन नैतिक दुविधाओं को संतुलित करना और परिवहन में एआई के लिए उचित नियम और दिशानिर्देश विकसित करना एक जटिल और निरंतर चुनौती है।

निष्कर्ष

हालाँकि एआई विभिन्न क्षेत्रों में महत्वपूर्ण लाभ और परिवर्तनकारी क्षमता प्रदान करता है, इसके सीमाओं और चुनौतियों को पहचानना और उनका समाधान करना आवश्यक है। एआई के लाभों और नुकसानों दोनों पर विचार करने वाला संतुलित दृष्टिकोण हमें मानवता की मौलिक जरूरतों और मूल्यों को संरक्षित करते हुए एक स्थायी भविष्य का निर्माण करने में मदद कर सकता है।

मिट्टी

मिट्टी की कीमत सोने और हीरे से भी कई गुना अधिक है। अगर हम मिट्टी की रक्षा नहीं करेंगे और उसे नष्ट करेंगे, तो हम मिट्टी के साथ-साथ खुद को भी नष्ट कर देंगे। अगर पूरी दुनिया में अन्न, जल और रोजगार की कमी नहीं होती, तो कोई युद्ध नहीं होता, कोई आतंकवाद नहीं होता, और कोई गरीब नहीं होता।

अगर हम मिट्टी को नहीं बचा पाए, तो पूरी दुनिया नष्ट हो जाएगी।

मौजूदा स्थिति:

संयुक्त राष्ट्र के खाद्य और कृषि संगठन के मुताबिक, पूरी दुनिया के पास खेती के लिए केवल 60 साल बचे हैं और विश्व की खाद्यान्न आपूर्ति के लिए हर साल किसानों को 60 लाख हेक्टेयर नई उपजाऊ जमीन की आवश्यकता है।

समस्या:

प्रत्येक वर्ष 120 लाख हेक्टेयर जमीन रासायनिक मिश्रित खाद और उर्वरकों के प्रयोग से कृषि के लिए अनुपयुक्त हो रही है।

भारत में स्थिति:

भारत में सबसे बड़ी दुख की बात यह है कि हिंदू बहुल राष्ट्र होने के बावजूद गायों की हत्या हो रही है। अगर गायों को संरक्षण दिया जाए, तो उनके गोबर से स्वदेशी खाद का उत्पादन करके बिना किसी रासायनिक या उर्वरक के बंजर भूमि को भी उपजाऊ बनाया जा सकता है और अधिक पैदावार करके पूरी दुनिया के खाद्यान्न संकट को रोका जा सकता है।

वैश्विक दृष्टिकोण:

पूरी दुनिया इस समय चांद और अन्य ग्रहों पर जीवन तलाश रही है, लेकिन जो धरती हमारे पास है उसे बचाने का कोई प्रयास नहीं किया जा रहा है।

समाधान:

अगर गायों को संरक्षण मिलेगा, तो देश और दुनिया को संरक्षण मिलेगा। जैविक खाद्यान्न तथा जैविक बीज उपलब्ध हो पाएंगे, जिससे देश की गरीबी तो दूर होगी ही, साथ ही साथ 80% तक बीमारियां भी कम हो जाएंगी।

भारत में जैविक खेती: विकल्प और भविष्य

अब सवाल यह उठता है कि क्या पूरे भारत में जैविक खेती लुप्त हो जाएगी, या इसका कोई और विकल्प है?

भारतीय कृषि का वर्तमान परिदृश्य:

भारत में कुछ ऐसी खेती की जा सकती है जिससे उद्योगपति भी आकर्षित हों। बड़े उद्योगपति पूर्णतः सक्षम हैं, उनके पास जमीनें हैं, और वे खेती के लिए बड़ा निवेश कर सकते हैं। वे विशेष खेती कर 5 से 10 साल तक इंतजार कर सकते हैं। लेकिन भारतीय किसान इतने सक्षम नहीं हैं कि मुनाफे के लिए 5 साल इंतजार कर सकें।

समाधान:

क्या हम ऐसा कोई एग्रीकल्चर बिजनेस मॉडल तैयार कर सकते हैं जिससे उद्योगपति और किसान मिलकर नए भारत की नींव रख सकें?

जब से हमने 5G (गायत्री मंत्र, गीता, गुरु, गंगा, गाय माता) को छोड़ा, तब से हमारे देश ने दुनिया में अपनी विशिष्ट पहचान खो दी।

भारत की प्राचीन पारंपरिक कृषि प्रणाली में गाय के गोबर की खाद को सर्वोत्तम खाद माना जाता है। लेकिन आज, हिंदू बहुल राष्ट्र होने के बाद भी असंख्य निर्दोष गौ माताओं की हत्या करके मांस व्यापार को बढ़ावा दिया जा रहा है। जब तक बैलगाड़ी का प्रयोग था, तब तक बैलों को संरक्षण प्राप्त था। आधुनिकीकरण के कारण बैलगाड़ियों का प्रयोग कम होने लगा और बहुत अधिक संख्या में बैलों की हत्या होने लगी।

गायों को केवल दूध देने तक ही उपयोग में लाया जाता है, और जैसे ही गाय दूध देना बंद कर देती है, उसे कत्लखाने भेजने के लिए खुला छोड़ दिया जाता है। किसानों की संख्या भी बहुत कम हो गई है, इसलिए वे गाय को पहले की तरह नहीं रख पा रहे हैं और अब गोबर की खाद की जगह रासायनिक खादों का प्रयोग कर रहे हैं।

एक समाधान:

अगर हम फिर से पारंपरिक कृषि प्रणाली की ओर लौटते हैं, तो गौ माता की सुरक्षा संभव हो सकती है। वर्तमान गायों की कमी से गोबर की खाद की आपूर्ति पूर्ण नहीं हो पाएगी, लेकिन इसके लिए हमें प्रत्येक गांव में एक सार्वजनिक गौशाला का निर्माण करना होगा। इससे बैल, गाय, भैंस जैसे जानवर, जिनका किसान अब उपयोग नहीं कर पा रहे हैं, गौशाला में एकत्रित किए जा सकते हैं और उनके गोबर से खाद बनाई जा सकती है। इस खाद का प्रयोग खेती में करके उस गांव की खाद की आपूर्ति की जा सकती है।

सामूहिक प्रयास:

इस पहल से गाय-बैल जैसे जानवरों को संरक्षित किया जा सकता है और पारंपरिक जैविक खेती के माध्यम से अधिक मात्रा में उत्पादन और बीमारियों से बचा जा सकता है।

उद्योगपति और किसानों का सहयोग:

- बिजनेस मॉडल: उद्योगपतियों और किसानों के बीच साझेदारी की जा सकती है। उद्योगपति बड़े निवेश कर सकते हैं और किसान इस निवेश का उपयोग जैविक खेती के लिए कर सकते हैं।

- संयुक्त प्रयास: बड़े उद्योगपतियों द्वारा जैविक खेती को प्रोत्साहित करने के लिए भूमि, संसाधन और तकनीक मुहैया कराई जा सकती है।
- प्रशिक्षण और विकास: किसानों को जैविक खेती के लाभों और तरीकों के बारे में शिक्षित किया जा सकता है, जिससे वे इस प्रणाली को अपनाने के लिए प्रेरित हो सकें।

इस प्रकार, उद्योगपतियों और किसानों के संयुक्त प्रयास से हम जैविक खेती को पुनर्जीवित कर सकते हैं और एक स्वस्थ और समृद्ध भारत की नींव रख सकते हैं।

खेती के लिए मुख्यतः चार प्रमुख चीजों की आवश्यकता है जमीन, बीज, पानी और खाद जमीन और खाद के संदर्भ में विस्तृत व्याख्या दी गई है अब हम पूरे भारत में विश्व का सबसे बड़ा बीज बैंक बनाना चाहते हैं जिससे कि प्रत्येक किसान को निशुल्क बीज उपलब्ध हो तथा पानी फाउंडेशन जैसी संस्थाओं के साथ मिलकर प्रत्येक गांव में पानी की आपूर्ति करने का कार्य करना चाहते हैं। इन प्रयासों से हम भारत को पुनः मजबूत जैविक कृषि संपन्न देश बना सकते हैं।

Source

- Https://www.stephen-knapp.com/
- https://www.researchgate.net/
- https://en.wikipedia.org/wiki/List_of_Indian_inventions_and_discoveries
- https://books.google.com/
- And many spiritual books